Refresh and *Gladden* *My Spirit*

Prayers and Meditations from Bahá'í Scripture

Introduction by Pamela Brode

Bahá'í
PUBLISHING
Wilmette, Illinois

Bahá'í Publishing
415 Linden Avenue
Wilmette, Illinois 60091-2844

Copyright © 2002 by the National Spiritual Assembly
of the Bahá'ís of the United States
All rights reserved. Published 2002

Cover design by Proof Positive/Farrowlyne Associates, Inc.

Library of Congress Cataloging-in-Publication Data

Refresh and gladden my spirit : prayers and meditations
from Bahá'í scripture / introduction by Pamela Brode.
    p. cm.
   ISBN 10: 1-931847-00-2 (alk. paper)
   ISBN 13: 978-1-931847-00-1 (alk. paper)
   1. Bahai Faith—Prayer-books and devotions,
English. I. Brode, Pamela, 1948–

  BP380 .R44 2002
  297.9'3433—dc21

                  2001035643

Printed in the United States of America
on acid-free paper ∞

08   07   06   4   3   2

O God!
Refresh and gladden my spirit.
Purify my heart.
Illumine my powers.
I lay all my affairs in Thy hand.
Thou art my Guide and my Refuge.
I will no longer be sorrowful
and grieved;
I will be a happy and joyful being.
O God! I will no longer be
full of anxiety,
nor will I let trouble harass me.
I will not dwell on the
unpleasant things of life.

O God! Thou art more friend to me than
I am to myself.
I dedicate myself to Thee, O Lord.

—Bahá'í Scripture

Contents

Contents

Introduction

by Pamela Brode

Not too long ago I ran into a friend who looked miserable. I hadn't seen him in quite a while, and I wondered what had happened to make the man look so stressed and forlorn. As if reading my mind, he explained in a somewhat panicky voice, "I'm spiritually bankrupt! My wife left me. I suddenly find myself a single parent. My whole world has crashed. I don't know if I'm coming or going."

Trying to be sensitive to his pain and not wanting to sound preachy, I asked gently, "Have you tried praying? I've always found that to be a source of comfort to me."

His response surprised me. He said, "I really need to discipline myself. Prayer is the only thing that seems to be helping me right now. But I'm not used to praying. I forgot to pray this morning—that must be why I'm feeling so spiritually empty. It's difficult to remember to pray every day. I don't want to turn to alcohol, but it's hard to resist."

I later reflected on our conversation. It is interesting that my friend considers it "hard to resist" alcohol but requires "discipline" to turn to prayer. Perhaps that is one of the mysteries of life—that we all seem to need to work the hardest for those things that benefit our souls the most and bring us genuine happiness. It takes effort to develop new habits, but when we succeed the rewards can be immeasurable. I think my friend would agree.

A few days later I saw him again, and he actually sounded cheerful. I asked him if he had prayed that day, and in an upbeat tone he replied, "Yes, I did! In fact, I've been praying every morning. It's amazing! When I pray I feel better about myself and more in control."

If prayer is not already a part of our normal daily routine, we may at first require an extra measure of discipline to incorporate it. However, once that happens, if we are truly yearning for the nearness of God, we derive such bountiful pleasure from immersing ourselves in the sweet ecstasy of prayer that the mere thought of life without it becomes unimaginable.

What Is Prayer? Countless individuals throughout the ages have experienced the profound effects of prayer and have been moved to attempt to define and describe that experience. By its simplest definition prayer is talking to God in a spirit of love. Some have characterized it as a conversation with God. Others have defined it as a love song to God. Still others have characterized it as food for the soul. Many historians, theologians, and believers agree that prayer is the purest expression of religion. At the very least it is a significant and universal aspect of religion.

The sixteenth-century Spanish mystic Saint Teresa of Ávila refers to prayer as "an intimate friendship, a frequent conversation held alone with the Beloved." Sadhu Sundar Singh, a modern Christian mystic of India, asserts that praying is as important as breathing. Lebanese poet and philosopher Kahlil Gibran refers to prayer as "the expansion of yourself into the living ether." The philosopher William James once declared prayer to be "the very soul and essence of religion."[1] Bahá'í scripture explains the reason for our creation and suggests that the experience of prayer may bring to light the knowledge of God's eternal love for us:

> . . . Veiled in My immemorial being and in the ancient eternity of My essence, I knew My love for thee; therefore I created thee, have

engraved on thee Mine image and revealed to thee My beauty.

. . . I loved thy creation, hence I created thee. Wherefore, do thou love Me, that I may name thy name and fill thy soul with the spirit of life.

. . . Love Me that I may love thee. If thou lovest Me not, My love can in no wise reach thee.[2]

Why Pray? Turning to a higher power for assistance, protection, and reassurance is not only an appealing concept, it is also a universal and natural condition in all human beings from the time of birth. Shortly after leaving the womb, the first instinctive noises of a newborn are cries for help, which are usually soon quieted and pacified once the infant is in the loving arms of the mother. Unable at first to walk, crawl, or do much of anything on our own, we learn from the earliest stages of infancy to be dependent on others who are more powerful than we are.

As the child matures into adulthood, that instinctive need and yearning to turn to a higher power for assistance, protection, and reassurance never dies. Many who believe in God find their greatest comfort and solace when turning to Him in prayer. There is no limit to the number of prayers one may offer to God. When prayers are offered with love and sincerity, the flow of God's infinite love fills the soul, bringing a sense of peace and gladness to the heart.

Every human being is bestowed with the free will to choose to turn his or her heart toward the path of God. King David of Israel sang out to the Lord, "My soul thirsts for God." Saint Augustine offered the invocation, "Behold, Lord, my heart is before Thee. . . ." In the Koran Muḥammad declares, "I have surrendered myself to God."[3]

Bahá'í scripture affirms that it is a natural course for us to turn to our Creator in prayer: "'If one friend loves another, is it not natural that he should wish to say so? Though he knows that that friend is aware of his love, does he still not wish to tell him of it? . . . It is true that God knows the wishes of all hearts; but the impulse to pray is a natural one, springing from man's love to God.'"[4]

The Bahá'í Approach to Prayer. As in every major religion, prayer is an essential element of the Bahá'í Faith. The religion's founder, Bahá'u'lláh, authored more than one hundred books, offering a wealth of prayers and spiritual teachings on virtually every aspect of life. These works, along with the writings of his herald, known as the Báb, and of his son 'Abdu'l-Bahá, comprise Bahá'í scripture.* Bahá'í scripture is written with an eloquence and beauty that is reminiscent of the language found in the King James version of the Bible. This elevated, dignified style, found in all Bahá'í prayers, contrasts strongly with our usual manner of speech and thought. Though this style may at first require more effort on the part of the reader, those who make the effort soon find that the style reinforces a sense of reverence toward God and helps to elevate our souls and enhance the transcendent quality of our prayers.

Bahá'ís throughout the world enjoy access to hundreds of prayers written by Bahá'u'lláh, the

---

* "Bahá'u'lláh," meaning "The Glory of God" in Arabic, is the title by which Mírzá Ḥusayn-'Alí (1817–1892), the founder of the Bahá'í Faith, is known. "The Báb," meaning "The Gate" in Arabic, is the title by which Mírzá 'Alí-Muḥammad (1819–1852), the herald of Bahá'u'lláh and founder of the Bábí Faith, is known. "'Abdu'l-Bahá," meaning "Servant of Bahá" (literally "Servant of Glory"), is the title by which Bahá'u'lláh's eldest son and appointed successor, 'Abbas Effendi (1844–1921), is known.

Báb, and 'Abdu'l-Bahá, and these have been widely translated into hundreds of languages. Covering topics such as healing, marriage, spiritual growth, aid and assistance, children, unity, and protection, Bahá'í prayers celebrate the goodness of God and His wisdom, offer solace and opportunities for spiritual growth, and define a path for drawing closer to Him.

There are a few specific prayers that Bahá'ís are obliged to recite in particular instances or on particular occasions. Beyond these few, however, Bahá'ís are free to pray as they wish, using prayers that come from Bahá'í or other scripture and writings or praying spontaneously in their own words. Even so, many Bahá'ís find the beauty and potency of the prayers found in Bahá'í scripture to be preferable. All of the prayers found in *Refresh and Gladden My Spirit* come from Bahá'í scripture; however, they represent only a small number of the many Bahá'í prayers that have thus far been translated into English.

Bahá'í scripture prescribes the daily practice of both prayer and meditation. While prayers may be recited, chanted, or sung aloud, meditation is engaged in during silent contemplation. No particular technique of meditation is advocated;

however, the things we meditate on should lead to spiritual illumination and nearness to God. The act of meditation can be likened to a mirror. If we set earthly objects before the mirror, it will reflect them. If we contemplate mundane matters, we will find ourselves becoming more informed of mundane matters. However, if we turn the mirror upward to the heavens—toward God—our hearts and minds will reflect the light of God, and we will reflect heavenly realities.

Some adherents of religion who believe that complete renunciation of earthly possessions is the true path to spiritual enlightenment may turn to asceticism. Although Bahá'í scripture affirms the benefit of detachment from the material world, it also exhorts us to practice moderation in all things, urging us to avoid all practices of excess such as asceticism, mendicancy, monasticism, esotericism, fanaticism. In fact, Bahá'í scripture states, "'One hour's reflection is preferable to seventy years of pious worship.'"[5]

Thus moderation is desirable even in the exercise of prayer. Moreover, the duration of time spent in prayer is less significant than the purity of intent behind it: "The most acceptable prayer is the one offered with the utmost spirituality and radiance; its prolongation hath not been and is not beloved by God. The more detached and the purer the prayer, the more acceptable is it in the presence of God." Furthermore, Bahá'u'lláh writes, "Lay not upon your souls that which will weary them and weigh them down, but rather what will lighten and uplift them. . . ."[6]

Prayer can and should increase our capacity to enjoy and appreciate our blessings, both materially and spiritually. When we are mindful of the fact that we are spiritual beings who dwell in a physical world, and when we can acknowledge that all that is good on earth is provided by God, we are better able to use, enjoy, and be thankful for the bounties we have been given. Bahá'í scripture asserts, "Happy is the soul that seeketh . . . heavenly teachings, and blessed is the heart which is stirred and attracted by the love of God."[7] This happiness is surely one of the greatest benefits to be gained when we commune with God.

In daily life prayer plays an extremely important role for Bahá'ís, who are enjoined to pray twice daily, both in the morning and in the evening. Bahá'u'lláh has prescribed the daily recitation of an obligatory prayer, which is to be said during one's private devotions. The primary purpose of such prayers is to draw us into a closer communion with God and nearer to the love and knowledge of God. A believer is free to choose any one of the three obligatory prayers provided by Bahá'u'lláh specifically for this purpose.

The shortest of the three obligatory prayers offered in Bahá'í scripture consists of a single verse, which is recited once a day between noon and sunset. This deeply profound yet simple prayer not only explains the purpose of our creation but also reminds us of our human frailty and of our need to turn to our Creator:

> I bear witness, O my God, that Thou hast created me to know Thee and to worship Thee. I testify, at this moment, to my powerlessness and to Thy might, to my poverty and to Thy wealth.
>
> There is none other God but Thee, the Help in Peril, the Self-Subsisting.[8]

The Bahá'í writings explain that these three daily obligatory prayers are invested by God with a special potency and significance. When they are recited in a spirit of faith and confidence, they enable us to enter into a much closer communion with God. The practice of daily obligatory prayer is a common thread linking many different religions. According to the teachings of many holy texts, the sacred duty of reciting specific prayers every day helps us to better understand our relationship with God and the purpose for which we were created—to love and to serve God through deeds that will benefit humanity.

Bahá'í scripture suggests that privately communing with God is the purest form of prayer and that prayers offered in this manner have a powerful effect on ourselves as well as others: "Whoso reciteth, in the privacy of his chamber, the verses revealed by God, the scattering angels of the Almighty shall scatter abroad the fragrance of the words uttered by his mouth, and shall cause the heart of every righteous man to throb."[9]

While private devotions are an extremely important element of every Bahá'í's religious life, reciting prayers in private is not the only way that Bahá'ís pray and turn to God. In fact, at any Bahá'í occasion, be it small or large, prayer is often used to bring focus to a gathering, to remind individuals of their love for God, and, through Him, of their love for one another. Wherever Bahá'ís may reside, spiritual gatherings are an integral part of Bahá'í community life. These gatherings may take place in a house of worship, a home, or any quiet place where believers may come together to pray in reverence and inhale the fragrance of God's love.

However, a decorum of reverence should not be confused with a solemn and grim atmosphere. On the contrary, the best of spiritual gatherings are celebratory and joyful and often include devotional music that can be as richly diverse as the people who attend the gatherings. In their dealings with one another, Bahá'ís are exhorted to engage in a spirit of fellowship and unity, and the combination of prayer and music is undoubtedly a potent tool to help reach that condition.

Forms and Modes of Prayer. Since time immemorial, prayer has been associated with acts of invocation, petition, sacrifice, atonement, confession, salvation, praise and thanksgiving, adoration, meditation, communion, obligation, devotion and piety, obedience, and submission. Bahá'í scripture offers a wealth of prayers for virtually any situation and every aspect of life.

The concept of sacrifice is common to all religions, and the Bahá'í Faith is no exception. Bahá'í scripture prescribes the personal spiritual act of sacrifice. This may involve the sacrifice of ego, of greed, of attachment to prejudices, and of other obstacles that prevent us from drawing closer to

God. The following lines from a prayer of Bahá'u'lláh express the desire to make such sacrifices: "fix . . . mine eyes upon Thee, and rid me of all attachment to aught else except Thyself. Aid me to do what Thou desirest, and to fulfill what Thou pleasest."[10]

Numerous petitions for aid and assistance, tests and difficulties, protection, healing, marriage, expectant mothers, children and youth, and for many other situations in life can be found in Bahá'í scripture. Each of these prayers reminds us that when we ask for blessings or assistance from God, our motive should be to lighten our physical burdens so that we may be free to commune with our Creator. For example: "Give us our daily bread, and grant Thine increase in the necessities of life, that we may be dependent on none other but Thee, may commune wholly with Thee, may walk in Thy ways and declare Thy mysteries."[11]

Most of us, even if we rarely pray, are prone to turn to God when we are afflicted with physical or mental ailments and need healing. Bahá'í scripture offers prayers for both physical and spiritual healing that acknowledge God as the Divine Healer. One such prayer begins, "Thy name is my healing, O my God, and remembrance of Thee is my remedy." The use of logic and common sense regarding health and healing are promoted in Bahá'í scripture, and all who are ill are advised both to pray and to seek medical treatment by a competent physician: "There are two ways of healing sickness, material means and spiritual means. The first is by the treatment of physicians; the second consisteth in prayers offered by the spiritual ones to God and in turning to Him. Both means should be used and practiced."[12]

Bahá'í scripture prescribes that confession is to be offered solely to God, and to God alone. There is no penance in the Bahá'í teachings nor any clergy, and Bahá'u'lláh forbids his followers to seek absolution of their sins from another human being. Thus our relationship with God is entirely personal and sacred, and no one may judge the measure of sincerity of another's devotion to God. When we feel the need for confession, Bahá'í scripture urges us to ask forgiveness from God, for "such confession before people results in one's humiliation and abasement," and God "wisheth not the humiliation of His servants." Many Bahá'í prayers include a confessional element. For example: "O God, my God! I have turned in repentance unto Thee, and verily Thou art the Pardoner, the Compassionate."[13]

A great many prayers for forgiveness can be found in Bahá'í scripture, all of them offering assurance that God will forgive us if we repent and pray for forgiveness with wholehearted sincerity and humility. The following verse from a prayer by Bahá'u'lláh offers an example: "O God our Lord! Protect us through Thy grace from whatsoever may be repugnant unto Thee. . . . Pardon us for the things we have done and wash away our sins and forgive us with Thy gracious forgiveness."[14]

As we draw ever closer to God, we may pray simply to offer praise and thanksgiving for the many gifts and bestowals we have received from Him, indeed for our very existence. Bahá'í prayers are rich with praise for God and His attributes. For example: "O Thou Whose face is the object of the adoration of all that yearn after Thee, Whose presence is the hope of such as are wholly devoted to Thy will, Whose nearness is the desire of all that have drawn nigh unto Thy court, Whose countenance is the companion of those who have recognized Thy truth, Whose name is the mover of the souls that long to behold Thy face, Whose voice is the true life of Thy lovers, the words of Whose mouth are as the waters of life unto all who are in heaven and on earth!"[15]

The selfless act of intercession—that is, praying to God on behalf of others, whether for souls in this world or for the departed—reaps benefits for the individual who prays as well as for the one on whose behalf the prayer is offered. Praying for our family, for our friends, and for others connects hearts and strengthens unity. Often, through the power of prayer, dissensions are miraculously resolved, misunderstandings reconciled, troubles averted. One Bahá'í prayer begins, "O my God! O my God! Unite the hearts of Thy servants, and reveal to them Thy great purpose."[16]

The Power of Prayer. As a firsthand witness to the mysterious power of prayer, I feel compelled to share a personal story about an incident that occurred on one particularly dreary and cold night in New York City during the late autumn of 1992.

I was walking down an isolated street with two companions, searching for a restaurant, when suddenly we were accosted by a large, bulky man. The assailant was huge—his demeanor so intimidating that his presence seemed to impose a towering wall, making it impossible for the three of us to pass. In a low, hostile voice obviously intended to frighten us, he growled, "Give me your money!"

As I stood between my two friends and looked up at the big, angry man, my immediate instinct was to turn to God. I thought to myself, "If I say a prayer right now, two things can happen—either the prayer will work and we'll be protected; or if he kills me, at least the last words that come out of my mouth will be a prayer to God, which certainly must be a good thing."

And so I pulled my one hundred-pound body up to my full five-feet, one-inch height, held my head high, and looked straight up into the man's eyes, reciting loudly one of my favorite prayers from Bahá'í scripture: "Is there any Remover of difficulties save God? Say: Praised be God! He is God! All are His servants, and all abide by His bidding!"[17]

Before I was even halfway through this short prayer, the towering bandit raised his hands as if to shield his face and, in a state of apparent panic and fear, pleaded, "Okay! Okay!" and ran off as fast as he could. By this time I had completely forgotten to be afraid. Turning around to face the running man's back, I shouted, "Wait! You didn't hear the whole prayer!"

Neither of my companions said a word. Both looked at me in shock, silently urging me to leave the scene of the potential crime. Shortly after resuming our walk we discovered a warm, cozy restaurant in which we not only enjoyed a delicious meal, but also ran into friends with whom we shared our strange experience. We reflected on what had frightened the man so terribly to make him run off. We concluded that, whatever the man thought, felt, or saw, the incident was significant because it affirmed unequivocally, certainly to those of us who witnessed it, the power of prayer and faith.

Peoples of all backgrounds—regardless of religion, nationality, ethnicity, gender, or culture—who are believers in God and in the sanctity of prayer offer unwavering testament that prayer is answered in many forms and can provide both spiritual as well as material assistance, protection, healing, and guidance. Can there be any question that prayer nourishes our spiritual well-being, enabling our souls to endure with amazing fortitude the harshest and most brutal trials and difficulties? Oppressed and suffering peoples throughout the ages have testified that it was their prayers that preserved their human dignity and sanity, sustaining their souls with comfort, fortitude, and even a measure of joy.

Referring to the powerful significance of prayer in African American culture, historian and author Derrick Bell writes, "Long ago, the slave singers, by interweaving melody and lyric in songs of faith—the spirituals—were able to transcend the awful oppression that defined their lives. Embracing religion that was undergirded by this music helped slaves to be free in their own minds."[18]

When we turn to God with a personal cry for help as we face everyday tests and challenges, whether big or small, that lead to stress and anxiety, prayer can reduce our stress and help to uplift our spirits regardless of the causes of our everyday annoyances and afflictions. Furthermore, numerous studies have established that prayer and meditation are associated with many beneficial effects on our physical and mental health.

A discussion on the subject of prayer that I had not too long ago with a friend who is an obstetrician helps to illustrate this fact. With complete assurance my friend said, "Everyone prays all the time, but they just don't know it."

I looked at my friend, about to question his reasoning, but then it occurred to me that maybe he knows what he's talking about—after all, he is a doctor who delivers babies. I thought about the delivery room and the countless women he has seen through the years who were frightened, in pain, and crying for help. He said, "When they're crying for help, I know they aren't calling for me. They're calling for God. Some of them realize it, but I think a lot of them don't, which is too bad. The ones who know they're turning to God get through the ordeal a lot easier." Those who consciously call upon God seem to experience less pain and anxiety.

God's love is always there for us. South Africa's Archbishop Desmond Tutu reminds us of this fact. He writes, "God created you because God loved you. . . . God's love for you is infinite, perfect and eternal. And so, as we keep still in the presence of God, we luxuriate in this knowledge: that we are loved, that all we are, all we have is a gift, freely and generously bestowed."[19] Feeling our Creator's love for us fuels us, inspires us, sustains us, gladdens us, and gives us strength. Praying to God with a soulful heart of faith reduces stress and anxiety because it enables us to increase our awareness of our spiritual reality and purpose. In turn, understanding our spiritual reality and our purpose in life ennobles our perceptions, sentiments, and understanding, thereby empowering us with a degree of detachment, calm, and control in our response to whatever occurs in our daily lives.

This attitude of detachment from the circumstances of our lives implies neither asceticism nor apathy. On the contrary, when we love things in this world for the sake of God and humbly praise and thank God for our daily blessings, our ability to enjoy and genuinely appreciate them is enhanced. However, when we begin to love things of the material world to such a degree that they take possession of our hearts, we lose perspective on who we are and what is most important in life and fall prone to unhappiness and disappointment.

As we strive to maintain a balance between our physical lives and our spiritual lives, it is important to nourish our souls as much as we do our bodies. God has given us the land that bears fruit to eat, and we know we cannot deprive the body of the sustenance it needs if we are to maintain good health. Just as food must be consumed every day to nourish the body, daily prayer is essential to nourish the soul. When we fail to pray, we deprive our souls of spiritual sustenance. The Bahá'í writings explain, "It is the soul of man which has first to be fed. And this spiritual nourishment prayer can best provide."[20] Fortifying ourselves with spiritual nourishment empowers us to take control of our lives and manage varying situations with clarity of mind and a positive attitude.

Are Our Prayers Answered? There is a mystic connection in our relationship with God that allows us the privilege to turn to our beloved Creator and pray for aid and assistance. That connection grows deeper when our prayers are offered in the spirit of love and faith and, when in accordance with God's will, those prayers are answered. The answers are not always immediate, and they do not always come in the ways that we want or expect them to come. However, many a soul has borne witness to the miracle of God's mercy, protection, comfort, and aid in times of need.

Many Eastern religions prescribe the practice of daily meditation as a means to commune with God and to connect with our spirituality by entering into a state of silent, contemplative prayer. Such a practice can help us not only to attain a sense of peace, serenity, and true happiness, but it can also enable us to listen with an open heart for the answers to our prayers.

We may wonder at times if our prayers are answered. The Bahá'í writings say that God "answers the prayers of all His servants," and that all human beings are servants of God. Authors William and Madeline Hellaby write in *Prayer: A*

Bahá'í Approach, "Prayers are *always* answered, let us be sure of that; but it may seem that they are not, if by 'answered' we mean that God granted our requests. . . . if our lives are in harmony with God, He will answer *us*—that is, our spiritual need—though He may not always assent to our request. He always does answer in one of three ways, 'Yes,' 'No,' or 'Wait'; and His method is either that He will change the *circumstances,* or He will change *us.*"[21]

God's mercy is mysterious, and His love has no bounds. There is a healthy logic in trusting that God loves us more than we love ourselves and that He, in His infinite wisdom, knows what is best for us better than we do. Our prayers will be answered affirmatively when they are in accord with the will of God.

Does that include our prayers for those who are ill and in need of healing? Quite often such prayers are answered and good health is restored. However, there are many times when, regardless of the prayers that may be offered or the quality of the medical care, recovery does not occur. Bahá'í scripture explains,

The prayers which were revealed to ask for healing apply both to physical and spiritual healing. Recite them, then, to heal both the soul and the body. If healing is right for the patient, it will certainly be granted; but for some ailing persons, healing would only be the cause of other ills, and therefore wisdom doth not permit an affirmative answer to the prayer.

. . . The power of the Holy Spirit healeth both physical and spiritual ailments.[22]

Regardless of the condition of the physical body, the potential always exists for the soul to reap spiritual rewards. Offering prayers with trust in God provides comfort and solace to the sufferer and emboldens one to face trials with courage and a radiant spirit.

Prayer is an indispensable aspect of life and fortifies us against the onslaught of every test and trial. If we trust God to answer our prayers in whatever ways will benefit our souls, regardless of the outcome, we will be less prone to disappointment. We can take comfort in knowing that our suffering, when endured for the sake of God, will be compensated in the world of the spirit. Bahá'í scripture explains, ". . . the rewards of this life are the real luminous perfections which are realized in this world, and which are the cause of eternal life, for they are the very progress of existence."[23]

Nonetheless, according to Bahá'í belief, prayer must be combined with action; we cannot simply pray and expect God to do the rest. We are enjoined to pray, to believe wholeheartedly that God will aid us, and then to take action. In fact, the Bahá'í writings suggest that we live our lives like a prayer, seeking God's help and strength in all of our day-to-day actions: ". . . strive that your actions day by day may be beautiful prayers."[24]

Does Prayer Benefit the World? What is true of the life of the individual is also applicable in the life of human society. Spiritual leaders, scholars, scientists, physicians, and many others today are speaking openly and gathering at world conferences to address the importance of prayer in human life and to raise awareness of the need to incorporate spiritual solutions to the global issues plaguing the world of humanity such as prejudice, persecution, extreme poverty, the environment, and war.

The United Nations Educational Scientific and Cultural Organization (UNESCO) issued the following statement at a 1993 meeting: "We believe that peace is possible. We know that religion is not the sole remedy for all the ills of humanity, but it has an indispensable role to play in this most critical time."[25]

Pope John Paul II, who traveled across the globe, urging people everywhere to pray for world peace, said to a large gathering in Paris in August 1997, "Continue to contemplate God's glory and God's love, and you will receive the enlightenment needed to build 'the civilization of love,' to help our brothers and sisters, to see the world transfigured by God's eternal wisdom and love."[26]

Certainly no rational mind in contemporary society questions the necessity to employ physical action in the remedy of social ills. But a new emergence of spirit is awakening multitudes throughout the global community to the realization that spiritual solutions are required to eliminate hatred and inequity as well as to achieve peace, justice, unity, and true prosperity for all members of the human family.

Moreover, many today who are seekers of truth are noting a remarkable sameness in the spiritual messages of various world religions, regardless of the differences in traditions and customs. All major religions proclaim the belief in a Supreme Being, the practice of prayer as a means to commune with God, the tenet to live a virtuous life, and all promote the message of peace.

Bahá'í scripture offers prayers for peace and for the realization of the oneness of the human race, as in the following lines from a prayer of 'Abdu'l-Bahá: "O Thou kind Lord! Unite all. . . . so that they may see each other as one family and the whole earth as one home. May they all live together in perfect harmony. . . . O God! Raise aloft the banner of the oneness of mankind."[27]

Bahá'ís in the United States have been actively working to spread the spiritual message of the oneness of the human family since the early twentieth century, and in recent decades a growing number of religious leaders of every persuasion have been speaking forth about the critical need to incorporate prayer in efforts to eliminate racial prejudice.

The African American Baptist reverend Dr. Martin Luther King, Jr., was among the most beloved and effective spiritual leaders to champion the Civil Rights Movement in the United States during the twentieth century. Speaking eloquently to the masses, offering prayers in each of his talks, always mentioning the praise and love of God with heartfelt reverence, he fervently encouraged his followers to turn their hearts to the

Almighty Lord in prayer in their struggle for justice, peace, and righteousness.

After winning the Nobel Peace Prize in 1964, Dr. King said prophetically, ". . . Negroes of the United States of America are engaged in a creative battle to end the long night of racial injustice . . . when the years have rolled past and when the blazing light of truth is focussed on this marvelous age in which we live—men and women will know and children will be taught that we have a finer land, a better people, a more noble civilization—because these humble children of God were willing to suffer for righteousness' sake."[28] It is hard to imagine that those who struggled and suffered in the Civil Rights Movement would have accomplished as much as they did or that they would have been able to endure so nobly without prayer and without turning their hearts fully to God.

The Quest for Spiritual Growth. Has humanity progressed spiritually through the ages? We have certainly advanced physically; we are taller and healthier, and we live decades longer than generations before us did. We have also made considerable progress in the sciences, arts, and technology; because of advancements in transportation and communication, we are becoming more globally connected.

Have we also progressed spiritually? Our hunger to independently investigate spiritual truths, our personal yearning to explore and unravel divine mysteries in seeking nearness to God—are these signs of humanity's readiness to advance in a new stage of spiritual evolution? Traditionally, people have relied on members of the clergy to guide their spiritual paths. Bahá'í scripture, however, advocates the independent investigation of truth for every individual:

> In order to find truth we must give up our prejudices, our own small trivial notions; an open receptive mind is essential. If our chalice is full of self, there is no room in it for the water of life. The fact that we imagine ourselves to be right and everybody else wrong is the greatest of all obstacles in the path towards unity, and unity is necessary if we would reach truth, for truth is one.
>
> Therefore it is imperative that we should renounce our own particular prejudices and superstitions if we earnestly desire to seek the truth. Unless we make a distinction in our

minds between dogma, superstition and prejudice on the one hand, and truth on the other, we cannot succeed.[29]

As in other sacred texts, Bahá'í scripture promulgates the message that there is only one true God, the Creator of all humanity, and teaches that each of us attains heavenly bestowals through the twin duties of prayer and action. However, the teachings found in Bahá'í scripture offer certain unique distinctions.

The fundamental, pivotal principle of the Bahá'í Faith is unity, which promotes the message that all people are equal and loved in the sight of God and that all are members of one human family. Bahá'í scripture strongly promotes the message of the equality of women and men, the importance of education for all, the advancement of the arts and sciences, and the independent search for truth. Bahá'ís believe that as we make prayer a part of our daily lives, we receive the sustenance and strength to better develop those noble, spiritual qualities that God has bestowed on all of us. This empowers us to bring to life such lofty concepts and ideals as those already mentioned, which in turn improve our lives and the lives of those around us.

Spiritual Sustenance. Prayer is often referred to as spiritual food for the soul; however, for me, prayer is also like the air that I breathe. While it may be possible to survive for a few days without food and water, the body can live only a matter of minutes without air. My spiritual well-being is so dependent upon the love and nearness of God that a day or even an hour without prayer, whether it be spoken aloud or uttered inwardly in meditative thought, is a suffocating notion. Prayer enables me to inhale the sweet fragrance of God's unconditional love, fortifying, purifying, and breathing life into my soul. Without prayer my spiritual existence would asphyxiate and collapse, as would my body if it were deprived of air.

Prayer has long fascinated me. Perhaps this is because of an early childhood incident that convinced me I had witnessed a miracle as a result of prayer. I was about five years old at the time. I tripped on the top steps of a long stairway that led down to the hard, cold, uncarpeted concrete floor of the basement in our house. I began to tumble rapidly down the stairs, and my mother, who came running from the kitchen into the little alcove above the stairs, screamed when she saw me. I remember shouting, "Help me, God!" My eyes were tightly shut when, suddenly, I felt a strong hand grab my own, halting my descent in midair.

I was resting on the steps, trembling, with my knees tucked under me and my arm still raised high when I opened my eyes and saw that no one was holding my hand. Confused, I looked up to the top of the stairs at my mother, who was standing there, frozen in place, shocked and startled. She asked, "How did you stop from falling?" I said, "Someone grabbed my hand." Later, while hugging me and stroking my hair, my mother said very little, but clearly she was relieved and happy that I was not hurt. I remember her saying softly, "It was a miracle." The prayer that I had offered that day as I flew down the steps was simple but sincere, and I was certain that it had been answered.

That incident sparked within me an interest in God, religion, and the power of prayer that has intensified through the years. After becoming enamored with prayers from Bahá'í scripture as a youth, I began a fascinating, often exhilarating, if at times somewhat bumpy, spiritual journey. For the next several years I investigated the holy scriptures of Judaism, Hinduism, Buddhism, Christianity, and the Islamic Faith, and I learned to practice Transcendental Meditation and yoga. Each step that I took as a spiritual seeker served to reinforce my belief that there is only one God and one human family. This belief eventually led me back to studying Bahá'í scripture, in which I found not only poetic beauty, spiritual sustenance, solace, strength, contentment, inspiration, and peace, but also—through prayer—a profound awakening of the love of God.

As you turn the pages of this book and read the prayers and meditations within it, think about them and ponder their meaning. Allow yourself to be drawn to the source of their inspiration—the Creator, our Heavenly Father, the one God of all the universe. Delight in the knowledge that God created you because He loves you. Allow yourself to luxuriate in God's love. May you find comfort. May you find peace. May you find happiness.

Enjoy your spiritual journey, and may God bless you and refresh and gladden your spirit.

Refresh and Gladden My Spirit

Prayers and Meditations
from Bahá'í Scripture

NOTE ON THE USE OF PRONOUNS

The Bahá'í scriptures were written in the Persian and Arabic languages. The translation of these writings into English frequently requires the use of the masculine pronouns "he" and "his" and words such as "man" and "men" in a generic, rather than gender-specific, sense. Bahá'í scripture explains, "Man is a generic term applying to all humanity. . . . In Persian and Arabic there are two distinct words translated into English as man: one meaning man and woman collectively, the other distinguishing man as male from woman the female. The first word and its pronoun are generic, collective; the other is restricted to the male."—ED.

Accepting God's Will

MEDITATIONS

Close thine eyes to all things else, and open them to the realm of the All-Glorious. Ask whatsoever thou wishest of Him alone; seek whatsoever thou seekest from Him alone. With a look He granteth a hundred thousand hopes, with a glance He healeth a hundred thousand incurable ills, with a nod He layeth balm on every wound, with a glimpse He freeth the hearts from the shackles of grief. He doeth as He doeth, and what recourse have we? He carrieth out His Will, He ordaineth what He pleaseth. Then better for thee to bow down thy head in submission, and put thy trust in the All-Merciful Lord.   1

Life afflicts us with very severe trials sometimes, but we must always remember that when we accept patiently the will of God He compensates us in other ways. With faith and love we must be patient, and He will surely reward us.   2

PRAYERS

I give praise to Thee, O my God, that the fragrance of Thy loving-kindness hath enraptured me, and the gentle winds of Thy mercy have inclined me in the direction of Thy bountiful favors. Make me to quaff, O my Lord, from the fingers of Thy bounteousness the living waters which have enabled every one that hath partaken of them to rid himself of all attachment to any one save Thee, and to soar into the atmosphere of detachment from all Thy creatures, and to fix his gaze upon Thy loving providence and Thy manifold gifts.

Make me ready, in all circumstances, O my Lord, to serve Thee and to set myself towards the adored sanctuary of Thy Revelation and of Thy Beauty. If it be Thy pleasure, make me to grow as a tender herb in the meadows of Thy grace, that the gentle winds of Thy will may stir me up and bend me into conformity with Thy pleasure, in such wise that my movement and my stillness may be wholly directed by Thee.

Thou art He, by Whose name the Hidden Secret was divulged, and the Well-Guarded Name was revealed, and the seals of the sealed-up Gob-

4

let were opened, shedding thereby its fragrance over all creation, whether of the past or of the future. He who was athirst, O my Lord, hath hasted to attain the living waters of Thy grace, and the wretched creature hath yearned to immerse himself beneath the ocean of Thy riches.

I swear by Thy glory, O Lord the Beloved of the world and the Desire of all them that have recognized Thee! I am sore afflicted by the grief of my separation from Thee, in the days when the Day-Star of Thy presence hath shed its radiance upon Thy people. Write down, then, for me the recompense decreed for such as have gazed on Thy face, and have, by Thy leave, gained admittance into the court of Thy throne, and have, at Thy bidding, met Thee face to face.

I implore Thee, O my Lord, by Thy name the splendors of which have encompassed the earth and the heavens, to enable me so to surrender my will to what Thou hast decreed in Thy Tablets, that I may cease to discover within me any desire except what Thou didst desire through the power of Thy sovereignty, and any will save what Thou didst destine for me by Thy will.

Whither shall I turn, O my God, powerless as I am to discover any other way except the way Thou didst set before Thy chosen Ones? All the atoms of the earth proclaim Thee to be God, and testify that there is none other God besides Thee. Thou hast from eternity been powerful to do what Thou hast willed, and to ordain what Thou hast pleased.

Do Thou destine for me, O my God, what will set me, at all times, towards Thee, and enable me to cleave continually to the cord of Thy grace, and to proclaim Thy name, and to look for whatsoever may flow down from Thy pen. I am poor and desolate, O my Lord, and Thou art the All-Possessing, the Most High. Have pity, then, upon me through the wonders of Thy mercy, and send down upon me, every moment of my life, the things wherewith Thou hast re-created the hearts of all Thy creatures who have recognized Thy unity, and of all Thy people who are wholly devoted to Thee.

Thou, verily, art the Almighty, the Most Exalted, the All-Knowing, the All-Wise.   3

Praised and glorified art Thou, O God! Grant that the day of attaining Thy holy presence may be fast approaching. Cheer our hearts through the potency of Thy love and good-pleasure, and bestow upon us steadfastness that we may willingly submit to Thy Will and Thy Decree. Verily, Thy knowledge embraceth all the things Thou hast created or wilt create, and Thy celestial might transcendeth whatsoever Thou hast called or wilt call into being. There is none to be worshiped but Thee, there is none to be desired except Thee, there is none to be adored besides Thee and there is naught to be loved save Thy good-pleasure.

Verily, Thou art the supreme Ruler, the Sovereign Truth, the Help in Peril, the Self-Subsisting. 4

Children

MEDITATIONS

Children are even as a branch that is fresh and green; they will grow up in whatever way ye train them. Take the utmost care to give them high ideals and goals, so that once they come of age, they will cast their beams like brilliant candles on the world. . . . 1

From the very beginning, the children must receive divine education and must continually be reminded to remember their God. Let the love of God pervade their inmost being, commingled with their mother's milk. 2

PRAYERS

Praised be Thou, O Lord my God! Graciously grant that this infant be fed from the breast of Thy tender mercy and loving providence and be nourished with the fruit of Thy celestial trees. Suffer him not to be committed to the care of anyone save Thee, inasmuch as Thou, Thyself, through the potency of Thy sovereign will and power, didst create and call him into being. There is none other God but Thee, the Almighty, the All-Knowing.

Lauded art Thou, O my Best Beloved, waft over him the sweet savors of Thy transcendent bounty and the fragrances of Thy holy bestowals. Enable him then to seek shelter beneath the shadow of Thy most exalted Name, O Thou Who holdest in Thy grasp the kingdom of names and attributes. Verily, Thou art potent to do what Thou willest, and Thou art indeed the Mighty, the Exalted, the Ever-Forgiving, the Gracious, the Generous, the Merciful.   3

Thou art He, O my God, through Whose names the sick are healed and the ailing are restored, and the thirsty are given drink, and the sore-vexed are tranquilized, and the wayward are guided, and the abased are exalted, and the poor are enriched, and the ignorant are enlightened, and the gloomy are illumined, and the sorrowful are cheered, and the chilled are warmed, and the downtrodden are raised up. Through Thy name, O my God, all created things were stirred up, and the heavens were spread, and the earth was established, and the clouds were raised and made to rain upon the earth. This, verily, is a token of Thy grace unto all Thy creatures.

I implore Thee, therefore, by Thy name through which Thou didst manifest Thy Godhead, and didst exalt Thy Cause above all creation, and by each of Thy most excellent titles and most august attributes, and by all the virtues wherewith Thy transcendent and most exalted Being is extolled, to send down this night from the clouds of Thy mercy the rains of Thy healing upon this suckling, whom Thou hast related unto Thine all-glorious Self in the kingdom of Thy creation. Clothe him, then, O my God, by Thy grace, with the robe of well-being and health, and guard him, O my Beloved, from every affliction and disorder, and from whatever is obnoxious unto Thee. Thy might, verily, is equal to all things. Thou, in truth, art the Most Powerful, the Self-Subsisting. Send down, moreover, upon him, O my God, the good of this world and of the next, and the good of the former and latter generations. Thy might and Thy wisdom are, verily, equal unto this.   4

O Thou peerless Lord! Let this suckling babe be nursed from the breast of Thy loving-kindness, guard it within the cradle of Thy safety and protection and grant that it be reared in the arms of Thy tender affection.   5

O God! Rear this little babe in the bosom of Thy love, and give it milk from the breast of Thy Providence. Cultivate this fresh plant in the rose garden of Thy love and aid it to grow through the showers of Thy bounty. Make it a child of the kingdom, and lead it to Thy heavenly realm. Thou art powerful and kind, and Thou art the Bestower, the Generous, the Lord of surpassing bounty.   6

O God! Educate these children. These children are the plants of Thine orchard, the flowers of Thy meadow, the roses of Thy garden.

Let Thy rain fall upon them; let the Sun of Reality shine upon them with Thy love. Let Thy breeze refresh them in order that they may be trained, grow and develop, and appear in the utmost beauty. Thou art the Giver. Thou art the Compassionate.   7

O Thou kind Lord! These lovely children are the handiwork of the fingers of Thy might and the wondrous signs of Thy greatness. O God! Protect these children, graciously assist them to be educated and enable them to render service to the world of humanity. O God! These children are pearls, cause them to be nurtured within the shell of Thy loving-kindness.

Thou art the Bountiful, the All-Loving.   8

O Lord! Make these children excellent plants. Let them grow and develop in the Garden of Thy Covenant, and bestow freshness and beauty through the outpourings of the clouds of the Abhá Kingdom.*

O Thou kind Lord! I am a little child, exalt me by admitting me to the kingdom. I am earthly,

---

* Literally, "the Most Glorious Kingdom": the spiritual world beyond this world.

make me heavenly; I am of the world below, let me belong to the realm above; gloomy, suffer me to become radiant; material, make me spiritual, and grant that I may manifest Thine infinite bounties.

Thou art the Powerful, the All-Loving.   9

O my Lord! O my Lord! I am a child of tender years. Nourish me from the breast of Thy mercy, train me in the bosom of Thy love, educate me in the school of Thy guidance and develop me under the shadow of Thy bounty. Deliver me from darkness, make me a brilliant light; free me from unhappiness, make me a flower of the rose garden; suffer me to become a servant of Thy threshold and confer upon me the disposition and nature of the righteous; make me a cause of bounty to the human world, and crown my head with the diadem of eternal life.

Verily, Thou art the Powerful, the Mighty, the Seer, the Hearer.   10

O Peerless Lord! Be Thou a shelter for this poor child and a kind and forgiving Master unto this erring and unhappy soul. O Lord! Though we are but worthless plants, yet we belong to Thy garden of roses. Though saplings without leaves and blossoms, yet we are a part of Thine orchard. Nurture this plant then through the outpourings of the clouds of Thy tender mercy and quicken and refresh this sapling through the reviving breath of Thy spiritual springtime. Suffer him to become heedful, discerning and noble, and grant that he may attain eternal life and abide in Thy Kingdom for evermore.   11

O Thou most glorious Lord! Make this little maidservant of Thine blessed and happy; cause her to be cherished at the threshold of Thy oneness, and let her drink deep from the cup of Thy love so that she may be filled with rapture and ecstasy and diffuse sweet-scented fragrance. Thou art the Mighty and the Powerful, and Thou art the All-Knowing, the All-Seeing.   12

Comfort

MEDITATION

If sorrow and adversity visit us, let us turn our faces to the Kingdom and heavenly consolation will be outpoured.

If we are sick and in distress let us implore God's healing, and He will answer our prayer.

When our thoughts are filled with the bitterness of this world, let us turn our eyes to the sweetness of God's compassion and He will send us heavenly calm! 1

PRAYERS

O Lord! Thou art the Remover of every anguish and the Dispeller of every affliction. Thou art He Who banisheth every sorrow and setteth free every slave, the Redeemer of every soul. O Lord! Grant deliverance through Thy mercy, and reckon me among such servants of Thine as have gained salvation.　　　2

Remove not, O Lord, the festal board that hath been spread in Thy Name, and extinguish not the burning flame that hath been kindled by Thine unquenchable fire. Withhold not from flowing that living water of Thine that mur-mureth with the melody of Thy glory and Thy remembrance, and deprive not Thy servants from the fragrance of Thy sweet savors breathing forth the perfume of Thy love.

Lord! Turn the distressing cares of Thy holy ones into ease, their hardship into comfort, their abasement into glory, their sorrow into blissful joy, O Thou that holdest in Thy grasp the reins of all mankind!

Thou art, verily, the One, the Single, the Mighty, the All-Knowing, the All-Wise.　　　3

Contentment

MEDITATIONS

The source of all good is trust in God, submission unto His command, and contentment with His holy will and pleasure. . . .

The source of all glory is acceptance of whatsoever the Lord hath bestowed, and contentment with that which God hath ordained. **1**

You see all round you proofs of the inadequacy of material things—how joy, comfort, peace and consolation are not to be found in the transitory things of the world. Is it not then foolishness to refuse to seek these treasures where they may be found? The doors of the spiritual Kingdom are open to all, and without is absolute darkness. **2**

PRAYERS

He is the Gracious, the All-Bountiful!
O God, my God! Thy call hath attracted me, and the voice of Thy Pen of Glory awakened me. The stream of Thy holy utterance hath enraptured me, and the wine of Thine inspiration entranced me. Thou seest me, O Lord, detached from all things but Thee, clinging to the cord of Thy bounty and craving the wonders of Thy grace. I ask Thee, by the eternal billows of Thy loving-kindness and the shining lights of Thy tender care and favor, to grant that which shall draw me nigh unto Thee and make me rich in Thy wealth. My tongue, my pen, my whole being, testify to Thy power, Thy might, Thy grace and Thy bounty, that Thou art God and there is none other God but Thee, the Powerful, the Mighty.

I bear witness at this moment, O my God, to my helplessness and Thy sovereignty, my feebleness and Thy power. I know not that which profiteth me or harmeth me; Thou art, verily, the All-Knowing, the All-Wise. Do Thou decree for me, O Lord, my God, and my Master, that which will make me feel content with Thine eternal decree and will prosper me in every world of Thine. Thou art in truth the Gracious, the Bountiful.

Lord! Turn me not away from the ocean of Thy wealth and the heaven of Thy mercy, and ordain for me the good of this world and hereafter. Verily, Thou art the Lord of the mercy-seat, enthroned in the highest; there is none other God but Thee, the One, the All-Knowing, the All-Wise.   3

O Lord! Unto Thee I repair for refuge, and toward all Thy signs I set my heart.

O Lord! Whether traveling or at home, and in my occupation or in my work, I place my whole trust in Thee.

Grant me then Thy sufficing help so as to make me independent of all things, O Thou Who art unsurpassed in Thy mercy!

Bestow upon me my portion, O Lord, as Thou pleasest, and cause me to be satisfied with whatsoever Thou hast ordained for me.

Thine is the absolute authority to command. 4

The Departed

MEDITATIONS

Death proffereth unto every confident believer the cup that is life indeed. It bestoweth joy, and is the bearer of gladness. It conferreth the gift of everlasting life. 1

Know thou of a truth that the soul, after its separation from the body, will continue to progress until it attaineth the presence of God. . . . 2

The spirit is changeless, indestructible. The progress and development of the soul, the joy and sorrow of the soul, are independent of the physical body. 3

The very fact that our spiritual instinct, surely never given in vain, prompts us to pray for the welfare of those, our loved ones, who have passed out of the material world: does it not bear witness to the continuance of their existence? 4

PRAYERS

Glory be to Thee, O Lord my God! Abase not him whom Thou hast exalted through the power of Thine everlasting sovereignty, and remove not far from Thee him whom Thou hast caused to enter the tabernacle of Thine eternity. Wilt Thou cast away, O my God, him whom Thou hast overshadowed with Thy Lordship, and wilt Thou turn away from Thee, O my Desire, him to whom Thou hast been a refuge? Canst Thou degrade him whom Thou hast uplifted, or forget him whom Thou didst enable to remember Thee?

Glorified, immensely glorified art Thou! Thou art He Who from everlasting hath been the King of the entire creation and its Prime Mover, and Thou wilt to everlasting remain the Lord of all created things and their Ordainer. Glorified art Thou, O my God! If Thou ceasest to be merciful unto Thy servants, who, then, will show mercy unto them; and if Thou refusest to succor Thy loved ones, who is there that can succor them?

Glorified, immeasurably glorified art Thou! Thou art adored in Thy truth, and Thee do we

all, verily, worship; and Thou art manifest in Thy
justice, and to Thee do we all, verily, bear witness. Thou art, in truth, beloved in Thy grace.
No God is there but Thee, the Help in Peril, the
Self-Subsisting.   5

O my God! O Thou forgiver of sins, bestower
of gifts, dispeller of afflictions!

Verily, I beseech Thee to forgive the sins of
such as have abandoned the physical garment and
have ascended to the spiritual world.

O my Lord! Purify them from trespasses, dispel their sorrows, and change their darkness into
light. Cause them to enter the garden of happiness, cleanse them with the most pure water, and
grant them to behold Thy splendors on the lofti-
est mount.   6

O my God! O my God! Verily, Thy servant,
humble before the majesty of Thy divine
supremacy, lowly at the door of Thy oneness, hath
believed in Thee and in Thy verses, hath testified
to Thy word, hath been enkindled with the fire
of Thy love, hath been immersed in the depths
of the ocean of Thy knowledge, hath been attracted by Thy breezes, hath relied upon Thee,

hath turned his face to Thee, hath offered his supplications to Thee, and hath been assured of Thy pardon and forgiveness. He hath abandoned this mortal life and hath flown to the kingdom of immortality, yearning for the favor of meeting Thee.

O Lord, glorify his station, shelter him under the pavilion of Thy supreme mercy, cause him to enter Thy glorious paradise, and perpetuate his existence in Thine exalted rose garden, that he may plunge into the sea of light in the world of mysteries.

Verily, Thou art the Generous, the Powerful, the Forgiver and the Bestower.   **7**

Detachment

MEDITATION

Be not troubled in poverty nor confident in riches, for poverty is followed by riches, and riches are followed by poverty. Yet to be poor in all save God is a wondrous gift, belittle not the value thereof, for in the end it will make thee rich in God. . . .   1

Our greatest efforts must be directed towards detachment from the things of the world; we must strive to become more spiritual, more luminous, to follow the counsel of the Divine Teaching, to serve the cause of unity and true equality, to be merciful, to reflect the love of the Highest on all . . . so that the light of the Spirit shall be apparent in all our deeds, to the end that all humanity shall be united, the stormy sea thereof calmed, and all rough waves disappear from off the surface of life's ocean henceforth unruffled and peaceful.   2

PRAYERS

Say: God sufficeth all things above all things, and nothing in the heavens or in the earth but God sufficeth. Verily, He is in Himself the Knower, the Sustainer, the Omnipotent.   **3**

O my God, my Lord and my Master! I have detached myself from my kindred and have sought through Thee to become independent of all that dwell on earth and ever ready to receive that which is praiseworthy in Thy sight. Bestow on me such good as will make me independent of aught else but Thee, and grant me an ampler share of Thy boundless favors. Verily, Thou art the Lord of grace abounding.   **4**

O my God! O my God! Glory be unto Thee for that Thou hast confirmed me to the confession of Thy oneness, attracted me unto the word of Thy singleness, enkindled me by the fire of Thy love, and occupied me with Thy mention and the service of Thy friends and maidservants.

O Lord, help me to be meek and lowly, and strengthen me in severing myself from all things and in holding to the hem of the garment of Thy glory, so that my heart may be filled with Thy love and leave no space for love of the world and attachment to its qualities.

O God! Sanctify me from all else save Thee, purge me from the dross of sins and transgressions, and cause me to possess a spiritual heart and conscience.

Verily, Thou art merciful and, verily, Thou art the Most Generous, Whose help is sought by all men.   5

Difficult Times

MEDITATIONS

Rely upon God. Trust in Him. Praise Him, and call Him continually to mind. He verily turneth trouble into ease, and sorrow into solace, and toil into utter peace. He verily hath dominion over all things. 1

Suffering is both a reminder and a guide. It stimulates us better to adapt ourselves to our environmental conditions, and thus leads the way to self improvement. In every suffering one can find a meaning and a wisdom. But it is not always easy to find the secret of that wisdom. It is sometimes only when all our suffering has passed that we become aware of its usefulness. What man considers to be evil turns often to be a cause of infinite blessings. And this is due to his desire to know more than he can. God's wisdom is, indeed, inscrutable to us all, and it is no use pushing too far trying to discover that which shall always remain a mystery to our mind. 2

PRAYERS

Lauded and glorified art Thou, O my God! I entreat Thee by the sighing of Thy lovers and by the tears shed by them that long to behold Thee, not to withhold from me Thy tender mercies in Thy Day, nor to deprive me of the melodies of the Dove that extolleth Thy oneness before the light that shineth from Thy face. I am the one who is in misery, O God! Behold me cleaving fast to Thy Name, the All-Possessing. I am the one who is sure to perish; behold me clinging to Thy Name, the Imperishable. I implore Thee, therefore, by Thy Self, the Exalted, the Most High, not to abandon me unto mine own self and unto the desires of a corrupt inclination. Hold Thou my hand with the hand of Thy power, and deliver me from the depths of my fancies and idle imaginings, and cleanse me of all that is abhorrent unto Thee.

Cause me, then, to turn wholly unto Thee, to put my whole trust in Thee, to seek Thee as my Refuge, and to flee unto Thy face. Thou art, verily, He Who, through the power of His might, doeth whatsoever He desireth, and commandeth, through the potency of His will, whatsoever He chooseth. None can withstand the operation of Thy decree; none can divert the course of Thine appointment. Thou art, in truth, the Almighty, the All-Glorious, the Most Bountiful.   3

O Thou Whose tests are a healing medicine to such as are nigh unto Thee, Whose sword is the ardent desire of all them that love Thee, Whose dart is the dearest wish of those hearts that yearn after Thee, Whose decree is the sole hope of them that have recognized Thy truth! I implore Thee, by Thy divine sweetness and by the splendors of the glory of Thy face, to send down upon us from Thy retreats on high that which will enable us to draw nigh unto Thee. Set, then, our feet firm, O my God, in Thy Cause, and enlighten our hearts with the effulgence of Thy knowledge, and illumine our breasts with the brightness of Thy names.   4

Thou knowest full well, O my God, that tribulations have showered upon me from all directions and that no one can dispel or transmute them except Thee. I know of a certainty, by virtue of my love for Thee, that Thou wilt never cause tribulations to befall any soul unless Thou desirest to exalt his station in Thy celestial

Paradise and to buttress his heart in this earthly life with the bulwark of Thine all-compelling power, that it may not become inclined toward the vanities of this world. Indeed Thou art well aware that under all conditions I would cherish the remembrance of Thee far more than the ownership of all that is in the heavens and on the earth.

Strengthen my heart, O my God, in Thine obedience and in Thy love, and grant that I may be clear of the entire company of Thine adversaries. Verily, I swear by Thy glory that I yearn for naught besides Thyself, nor do I desire anything except Thy mercy, nor am I apprehensive of aught save Thy justice. I beg Thee to forgive me as well as those whom Thou lovest, howsoever Thou pleasest. Verily, Thou art the Almighty, the Bountiful.

Immensely exalted art Thou, O Lord of the heavens and earth, above the praise of all men, and may peace be upon Thy faithful servants and glory be unto God, the Lord of all the worlds. 5

O my God! There is no one but Thee to allay the anguish of my soul, and Thou art my highest aspiration, O my God. My heart is wedded to none save Thee and such as Thou dost love. I solemnly declare that my life and death are both for Thee. Verily Thou art incomparable and hast no partner.

O my Lord! I beg Thee to forgive me for shutting myself out from Thee. By Thy glory and majesty, I have failed to befittingly recognize Thee and to worship Thee, while Thou dost make Thyself known unto me and callest me to remembrance as beseemeth Thy station. Grievous woe would betide me, O my Lord, wert Thou to take hold of me by reason of my misdeeds and trespasses. No helper do I know of other than Thee. No refuge do I have to flee to save Thee. None among Thy creatures can dare to intercede with Thyself without Thy leave. I hold fast to Thy love before Thy court, and, according to Thy bidding, I earnestly pray unto Thee as befitteth Thy glory. I beg Thee to heed my call as Thou hast promised me. Verily Thou art God; no God is there but Thee. Alone and unaided, Thou art independent of all created things. Neither can the devotion of Thy lovers profit Thee, nor the evil doings of the faithless harm Thee. Verily Thou art my God, He Who will never fail in His promise.

O my God! I beseech Thee by the evidences of Thy favor, to let me draw nigh unto the sublime heights of Thy holy presence, and protect me from inclining myself toward the subtle allusions of aught else but Thee. Guide my steps, O my God, unto that which is acceptable and pleasing to Thee. Shield me, through Thy might, from the fury of Thy wrath and chastisement, and hold me back from entering habitations not desired by Thee.   6

Is there any Remover of difficulties save God? Say: Praised be God! He is God! All are His servants, and all abide by His bidding!   7

O my God! I have failed to know Thee as is worthy of Thy glory, and I have failed to fear Thee as befitteth my station. How can I make mention of Thee when I am in this condition, and how can I set my face towards Thee when I have fallen short of my duty in worshiping Thee?

Thou didst not call me into being to demonstrate the potency of Thy might which is unmistakably manifest and evident; for Thou art God Who everlastingly existed when there was naught. Rather Thou didst create us through Thy transcendent power that a bare mention may be graciously made of us before the resplendent manifestation of Thy Remembrance.

I have no knowledge of Thee, O my God, but that which Thou hast taught me whereby I might recognize Thy Self—a knowledge which reflecteth only my failure and sinfulness. Here am I then, O my God, wholly consecrated unto Thee, willing to do what Thou desirest. Humbly I cast myself before the revelations of Thy mercy, confessing that Thou art God, no God is there but Thee, and that Thou art incomparable, hast no partner and naught is there like Thee. Unto this Thou Thyself bearest witness, as well becometh Thy glory.   8

O God! O God! This is a broken-winged bird and his flight is very slow—assist him so that he may fly toward the apex of prosperity and salvation, wing his way with the utmost joy and happiness throughout the illimitable space, raise his melody in Thy Supreme Name in all the regions, exhilarate the ears with this call, and brighten the eyes by beholding the signs of guidance.

O Lord! I am single, alone and lowly. For me there is no support save Thee, no helper except Thee and no sustainer beside Thee. Confirm me in Thy service, assist me with the cohorts of Thy angels, make me victorious in the promotion of Thy Word and suffer me to speak out Thy wisdom amongst Thy creatures. Verily, Thou art the helper of the weak and the defender of the little ones, and verily Thou art the Powerful, the Mighty and the Unconstrained. 9

Evening

MEDITATIONS

Reflect, O people, on the grace and blessings of your Lord, and yield Him thanks at eventide and dawn.   1

The state of prayer is the best of conditions. . . . Prayer verily bestoweth life, particularly when offered in private and at times, such as midnight, when freed from daily cares.   2

Prayers

O my God, my Master, the Goal of my desire! This, Thy servant, seeketh to sleep in the shelter of Thy mercy, and to repose beneath the canopy of Thy grace, imploring Thy care and Thy protection.

I beg of Thee, O my Lord, by Thine eye that sleepeth not, to guard mine eyes from beholding aught beside Thee. Strengthen, then, their vision that they may discern Thy signs, and behold the Horizon of Thy Revelation. Thou art He before the revelations of Whose omnipotence the quintessence of power hath trembled.

No God is there but Thee, the Almighty, the All-Subduing, the Unconditioned.   3

How can I choose to sleep, O God, my God, when the eyes of them that long for Thee are wakeful because of their separation from Thee; and how can I lie down to rest whilst the souls of Thy lovers are sore vexed in their remoteness from Thy presence?

I have committed, O my Lord, my spirit and my entire being into the right hand of Thy might and Thy protection, and I lay my head on my pillow through Thy power, and lift it up according to Thy will and Thy good pleasure. Thou art, in truth, the Preserver, the Keeper, the Almighty, the Most Powerful.

By Thy might! I ask not, whether sleeping or waking, but that which Thou dost desire. I am Thy servant and in Thy hands. Do Thou graciously aid me to do what will shed forth the fragrance of Thy good pleasure. This, truly, is my hope and the hope of them that enjoy near access to Thee. Praised be Thou, O Lord of the worlds!   4

O Lord, I have turned my face unto Thy kingdom of oneness and am immersed in the sea of Thy mercy. O Lord, enlighten my sight by beholding Thy lights in this dark night, and make me happy by the wine of Thy love in this wonderful age. O Lord, make me hear Thy call, and open before my face the doors of Thy heaven, so that I may see the light of Thy glory and become attracted to Thy beauty.

Verily, Thou art the Giver, the Generous, the Merciful, the Forgiving.   5

Faith

MEDITATIONS

Place not thy reliance on thy treasures. Put thy whole confidence in the grace of God, thy Lord. Let Him be thy trust in whatever thou doest, and be of them that have submitted themselves to His Will.   1

The essence of faith is fewness of words and abundance of deeds; he whose words exceed his deeds, know verily his death is better than his life.   2

Oh, trust in God! for His Bounty is everlasting, and in His Blessings, for they are superb. Oh! put your faith in the Almighty, for He faileth not and His goodness endureth forever!   3

PRAYERS

O Thou Whose nearness is my wish, Whose presence is my hope, Whose remembrance is my desire, Whose court of glory is my goal, Whose abode is my aim, Whose name is my healing, Whose love is the radiance of my heart, Whose service is my highest aspiration! I beseech Thee by Thy Name, through which Thou hast enabled them that have recognized Thee to soar to the sublimest heights of the knowledge of Thee and empowered such as devoutly worship Thee to ascend into the precincts of the court of Thy holy favors, to aid me to turn my face towards Thy face, to fix mine eyes upon Thee, and to speak of Thy glory.

I am the one, O my Lord, who hath forgotten all else but Thee, and turned towards the Dayspring of Thy grace, who hath forsaken all save Thyself in the hope of drawing nigh unto Thy court. Behold me, then, with mine eyes lifted up towards the Seat that shineth with the splendors of the light of Thy Face. Send down, then, upon me, O my Beloved, that which will enable me to be steadfast in Thy Cause, so that the doubts of the infidels may not hinder me from turning towards Thee.

Thou art, verily, the God of Power, the Help in Peril, the All-Glorious, the Almighty.   4

O Lord my God! Assist Thy loved ones to be firm in Thy Faith, to walk in Thy ways, to be steadfast in Thy Cause. Give them Thy grace to withstand the onslaught of self and passion, to follow the light of divine guidance. Thou art the Powerful, the Gracious, the Self-Subsisting, the Bestower, the Compassionate, the Almighty, the All-Bountiful.   5

O compassionate God! Thanks be to Thee for Thou hast awakened and made me conscious. Thou hast given me a seeing eye and favored me with a hearing ear, hast led me to Thy kingdom and guided me to Thy path. Thou hast shown me the right way and caused me to enter the ark of deliverance. O God! Keep me steadfast and make me firm and staunch. Protect me from violent tests and preserve and shelter me in the strongly fortified fortress of Thy Covenant and Testament. Thou art the Powerful. Thou art the Seeing. Thou art the Hearing.

O Thou the Compassionate God. Bestow upon me a heart which, like unto a glass, may be illumined with the light of Thy love, and confer upon me thoughts which may change this world into a rose garden through the outpourings of heavenly grace.

Thou art the Compassionate, the Merciful. Thou art the Great Beneficent God.　　6

Forgiveness

MEDITATIONS

Verily in this Day all that dwell on earth are the servants of God. As to those who truly believe in God and are well assured in the signs revealed by Him, perchance He will graciously forgive them the things their hands have committed, and will grant them admission into the precincts of His mercy. He, in truth, is the Ever-Forgiving, the Compassionate.   1

Pray to God day and night and beg forgiveness and pardon. The omnipotence of God shall solve every difficulty.   2

PRAYERS

O God our Lord! Protect us through Thy grace from whatsoever may be repugnant unto Thee, and vouchsafe unto us that which well beseemeth Thee. Give us more out of Thy bounty, and bless us. Pardon us for the things we have done, and wash away our sins, and forgive us with Thy gracious forgiveness. Verily, Thou art the Most Exalted, the Self-Subsisting.

Thy loving providence hath encompassed all created things in the heavens and on the earth, and Thy forgiveness hath surpassed the whole creation. Thine is sovereignty; in Thy hand are the Kingdoms of Creation and Revelation; in Thy right hand Thou holdest all created things, and within Thy grasp are the assigned measures of forgiveness. Thou forgivest whomsoever among Thy servants Thou pleasest. Verily, Thou art the Ever-Forgiving, the All-Loving. Nothing whatsoever escapeth Thy knowledge, and naught is there which is hidden from Thee.

O God our Lord! Protect us through the potency of Thy might, enable us to enter Thy wondrous surging ocean, and grant us that which well befitteth Thee.

Thou art the Sovereign Ruler, the Mighty Doer, the Exalted, the All-Loving. 3

Praise be unto Thee, O Lord. Forgive us our sins, have mercy upon us and enable us to return unto Thee. Suffer us not to rely on aught else besides Thee, and vouchsafe unto us, through Thy bounty, that which Thou lovest and desirest and well beseemeth Thee. Exalt the station of them that have truly believed, and forgive them with Thy gracious forgiveness. Verily, Thou art the Help in Peril, the Self-Subsisting. 4

I beg Thee to forgive me, O my Lord, for every mention but the mention of Thee, and for every praise but the praise of Thee, and for every delight but delight in Thy nearness, and for every pleasure but the pleasure of communion with Thee, and for every joy but the joy of Thy love and of Thy good-pleasure, and for all things pertaining unto me which bear no relationship unto Thee, O Thou Who art the Lord of lords, He Who provideth the means and unlocketh the doors. 5

Glory be unto Thee, O God. How can I make mention of Thee while Thou art sanctified from the praise of all mankind. Magnified be Thy Name, O God, Thou art the King, the Eternal Truth; Thou knowest what is in the heavens and on the earth, and unto Thee must all return. Thou hast sent down Thy divinely ordained Revelation according to a clear measure. Praised art Thou, O Lord! At Thy behest Thou dost render victorious whomsoever Thou willest, through the hosts of heaven and earth and whatsoever existeth between them. Thou art the Sovereign, the Eternal Truth, the Lord of invincible might.

Glorified art Thou, O Lord! Thou forgivest at all times the sins of such among Thy servants as implore Thy pardon. Wash away my sins and the sins of those who seek Thy forgiveness at dawn, who pray to Thee in the daytime and in the night season, who yearn after naught save God, who offer up whatsoever God hath graciously bestowed upon them, who celebrate Thy praise at morn and eventide, and who are not remiss in their duties.   6

I am aware, O Lord, that my trespasses have covered my face with shame in Thy presence, and have burdened my back before Thee, have intervened between me and Thy beauteous countenance, have compassed me from every direc-

tion and have hindered me on all sides from gain-
ing access unto the revelations of Thy celestial
power.

O Lord! If Thou forgivest me not, who is there
then to grant pardon, and if Thou hast no mercy
upon me who is capable of showing compassion?
Glory be unto Thee, Thou didst create me when
I was non-existent and Thou didst nourish me
while I was devoid of any understanding. Praise
be unto Thee, every evidence of bounty pro-
ceedeth from Thee and every token of grace
emanateth from the treasuries of Thy decree. 7

O Thou forgiving Lord!
   Although some souls have spent the days
of their lives in ignorance, and became estranged
and contumacious, yet, with one wave from the
ocean of Thy forgiveness, all those encompassed
by sin will be set free. Whomsoever Thou willest
Thou makest a confidant, and whosoever is not
the object of Thy choice is accounted a trans-
gressor. Shouldst Thou deal with us with Thy
justice, we are all naught but sinners and deserv-
ing to be shut out from Thee, but shouldst Thou
uphold mercy, every sinner would be made pure
and every stranger a friend. Bestow, then, Thy

forgiveness and pardon, and grant Thy mercy unto all.

Thou art the Forgiver, the Lightgiver and the Omnipotent.   8

O Lord! Look not at our shortcomings. Deal with us according to Thy grace and bounty. Our shortcomings are many, but the ocean of Thy forgiveness is boundless. Our weakness is grievous, but the evidences of Thine aid and assistance are clear. Therefore, confirm and strengthen us. Enable us to do that which is worthy of Thy holy Threshold. Illumine our hearts, grant us discerning eyes and attentive ears. Resuscitate the dead and heal the sick. Bestow wealth upon the poor and give peace and security to the fearful. Accept us in Thy kingdom and illumine us with the light of guidance. Thou art the Powerful and the Omnipotent. Thou art the Generous. Thou art the Clement. Thou art the Kind.   9

Guidance and Inspiration

MEDITATIONS

Only when the lamp of search, of earnest striving, of longing desire, of passionate devotion, of fervid love, of rapture, and ecstasy, is kindled within the seeker's heart, and the breeze of His [God's] loving-kindness is wafted upon his soul, will the darkness of error be dispelled, the mists of doubts and misgivings be dissipated, and the lights of knowledge and certitude envelop his being. . . . Then will the manifold favors and outpouring grace of the holy and everlasting Spirit confer such new life upon the seeker that he will find himself endowed with a new eye, a new ear, a new heart, and a new mind. 1

He [God], verily, will aid every one that aideth Him, and will remember every one that remembereth Him. 2

PRAYERS

Magnified be Thy Name, O Lord my God! I am the one who hath turned his face towards Thee and hath placed his whole reliance in Thee. I implore Thee by Thy Name whereby the ocean of Thine utterance hath surged and the breezes of Thy knowledge have stirred, to grant that I may be graciously aided to serve Thy Cause and be inspired to remember Thee and praise Thee. Send down then upon me from the heaven of Thy generosity that which will preserve me from anyone but Thee and will profit me in all Thy worlds.

Verily, Thou art the Powerful, the Inaccessible, the Supreme, the Knowing, the Wise.   3

O God, O Thou Who hast cast Thy splendor over the luminous realities of men, shedding upon them the resplendent lights of knowledge and guidance, and hast chosen them out of all created things for this supernal grace, and hast caused them to encompass all things, to understand their inmost essence, and to disclose their mysteries, bringing them forth out of darkness into the visible world! "He verily showeth His special mercy to whomsoever He will."*

O Lord, help Thou Thy loved ones to acquire knowledge and the sciences and arts, and to unravel the secrets that are treasured up in the inmost reality of all created beings. Make them to hear the hidden truths that are written and embedded in the heart of all that is. Make them to be ensigns of guidance amongst all creatures, and piercing rays of the mind shedding forth their light in this, the "first life."* Make them to be leaders unto Thee, guides unto Thy path, runners urging men on to Thy Kingdom.

Thou verily art the Powerful, the Protector, the Potent, the Defender, the Mighty, the Most Generous.   4

O God, guide me, protect me, make of me a shining lamp and a brilliant star. Thou art the Mighty and the Powerful.   5

---

* Koran 3:67.
* Koran 56:62.

Happiness

MEDITATIONS

Were a man to read a single verse with joy and radiance it would be better for him than to read with lassitude all the Holy Books of God, the Help in Peril, the Self-Subsisting. Read ye the sacred verses in such measure that ye be not overcome by languor and despondency. Lay not upon your souls that which will weary them and weigh them down, but rather what will lighten and uplift them, so that they may soar on the wings of the Divine verses towards the Dawning-place of His manifest signs; this will draw you nearer to God, did ye but comprehend.   1

Man is, in reality, a spiritual being, and only when he lives in the spirit is he truly happy.   2

Human happiness is founded upon spiritual behavior.   3

It is the wish of our heavenly Father that every heart should rejoice and be filled with happiness, that we should live together in felicity and joy. The obstacle to human happiness is racial or religious prejudice, the competitive struggle for existence and inhumanity toward each other.   4

PRAYERS

O God, my God! Thou art my Hope and my Beloved, my highest Aim and Desire! With great humbleness and entire devotion I pray to Thee to make me a minaret of Thy love in Thy land, a lamp of Thy knowledge among Thy creatures, and a banner of divine bounty in Thy dominion.

Number me with such of Thy servants as have detached themselves from everything but Thee, have sanctified themselves from the transitory things of this world, and have freed themselves from the promptings of the voicers of idle fancies.

Let my heart be dilated with joy through the spirit of confirmation from Thy kingdom, and brighten my eyes by beholding the hosts of divine assistance descending successively upon me from the kingdom of Thine omnipotent glory.

Thou art, in truth, the Almighty, the All-Glorious, the All-Powerful.   5

O God! Refresh and gladden my spirit. Purify my heart. Illumine my powers. I lay all my affairs in Thy hand. Thou art my Guide and my Refuge. I will no longer be sorrowful and grieved; I will be a happy and joyful being. O God! I will no longer be full of anxiety, nor will I let trouble harass me. I will not dwell on the unpleasant things of life.

O God! Thou art more friend to me than I am to myself. I dedicate myself to Thee, O Lord.   6

Healing

MEDITATIONS

Know thou that the soul of man is exalted above, and is independent of all infirmities of body or mind. That a sick person showeth signs of weakness is due to the hindrances that interpose themselves between his soul and his body, for the soul itself remaineth unaffected by any bodily ailments. 1

There are two ways of healing sickness, material means and spiritual means. The first is by the treatment of physicians; the second consisteth in prayers offered by the spiritual ones to God and in turning to Him. Both means should be used and practiced. 2

Prayers

Thy name is my healing, O my God, and remembrance of Thee is my remedy. Nearness to Thee is my hope, and love for Thee is my companion. Thy mercy to me is my healing and my succor in both this world and the world to come. Thou, verily, art the All-Bountiful, the All-Knowing, the All-Wise.   3

O God, my God! I beg of Thee by the ocean of Thy healing, and by the splendors of the Daystar of Thy grace, and by Thy Name through which Thou didst subdue Thy servants, and by the pervasive power of Thy most exalted Word and the potency of Thy most august Pen, and by Thy mercy that hath preceded the creation of all who are in heaven and on earth, to purge me with the waters of Thy bounty from every affliction and disorder, and from all weakness and feebleness.

Thou seest, O my Lord, Thy suppliant waiting at the door of Thy bounty, and him who hath set his hopes on Thee clinging to the cord of Thy generosity. Deny him not, I beseech Thee, the things he seeketh from the ocean of Thy grace and the Daystar of Thy loving-kindness.

Powerful art Thou to do what pleaseth Thee. There is none other God save Thee, the Ever-Forgiving, the Most Generous. **4**

Help and Assistance

MEDITATIONS

It behooveth the servant to pray to and seek assistance from God, and to supplicate and implore His aid. Such becometh the rank of servitude, and the Lord will decree whatsoever He desireth, in accordance with His consummate wisdom.　　1

Remember not your own limitations; the help of God will come to you. Forget yourself. God's help will surely come!

　　When you call on the Mercy of God waiting to reinforce you, your strength will be tenfold.　　2

The very act of striving to serve, however unworthy one may feel, attracts the blessings of God and enables one to become more fitted for the task.　　3

PRAYERS

O God my God! Thou seest me standing before the door of Thy forgiveness and benevolence, turning my gaze toward the horizon of Thy bountiful favors and manifold blessings. I beg of Thee by Thy sweet accents and by the shrill voice of Thy Pen, O Lord of all mankind, to graciously aid Thy servants as it befitteth Thy days and beseemeth the glory of Thy manifestation and Thy majesty. Verily potent art Thou to do whatsoever Thou willest. All they that dwell in the heavens and on the earth bear witness to Thy power and Thy might, to Thy glory and Thy bounteousness. Praise be to Thee, O Lord of the worlds and the Well-Beloved of the heart of every man of understanding!

Thou beholdest, O my God, the essence of poverty seeking the ocean of Thy wealth and the substance of iniquity yearning for the waters of Thy forgiveness and Thy tender mercy. Grant Thou, O my God, that which beseemeth Thy great glory and befitteth the loftiness of Thy boundless grace. Thou art in truth the All-Bountiful, the Lord of grace abounding, the Ordainer, the All-Wise. No God is there but

Thee, the Most Powerful, the All-Compelling, the Omnipotent. **4**

We pray to God to graciously assist them that have been led astray to be just and fair-minded, and to make them aware of that whereof they have been heedless. He, in truth, is the All-Bounteous, the Most Generous. Debar not Thy servants, O my Lord, from the door of Thy grace, and drive them not away from the court of Thy presence. Assist them to dispel the mists of idle fancy, and to tear away the veils of vain imaginings and hopes. Thou art, verily, the All-Possessing, the Most High. No God is there but Thee, the Almighty, the Gracious. **5**

In the Name of Thy Lord, the Creator, the Sovereign, the All-Sufficing, the Most Exalted, He Whose help is implored by all men.

Say: O my God! O Thou Who art the Maker of the heavens and of the earth, O Lord of the Kingdom! Thou well knowest the secrets of my heart, while Thy Being is inscrutable to all save Thyself. Thou seest whatsoever is of me, while no one else can do this save Thee. Vouchsafe unto me, through Thy grace, what will enable me to dispense with all except Thee, and destine for me that which will make me independent of everyone else besides Thee. Grant that I may reap the benefit of my life in this world and in the next. Open to my face the portals of Thy grace, and graciously confer upon me Thy tender mercy and bestowals.

O Thou Who art the Lord of grace abounding! Let Thy celestial aid surround those who love Thee, and bestow upon us the gifts and the bounties Thou dost possess. Be Thou sufficient unto us of all things, forgive our sins and have mercy upon us. Thou art Our Lord and the Lord of all created things. No one else do we invoke but Thee, and naught do we beseech but Thy favors. Thou art the Lord of bounty and grace, invincible in Thy power and the most skillful in Thy designs. No God is there but Thee, the All-Possessing, the Most Exalted.

Confer Thy blessings, O my Lord, upon the Messengers, the holy ones and the righteous. Verily, Thou art God, the Peerless, the All-Compelling.   6

G lory be to Thee, O God! Thou art the God Who hath existed before all things, Who will exist after all things and will last beyond all things. Thou art the God Who knoweth all things, and is supreme over all things. Thou art the God Who dealeth mercifully with all things,

Who judgeth between all things and Whose vision embraceth all things. Thou art God my Lord, Thou art aware of my position, Thou dost witness my inner and outer being.

Grant Thy forgiveness unto me and unto the believers who responded to Thy Call. Be Thou my sufficing helper against the mischief of whosoever may desire to inflict sorrow upon me or wish me ill. Verily, Thou art the Lord of all created things. Thou dost suffice everyone, while no one can be self-sufficient without Thee. 7

O Thou kind Lord! We are servants of Thy Threshold, taking shelter at Thy holy Door. We seek no refuge save only this strong pillar, turn nowhere for a haven but unto Thy safe-keeping. Protect us, bless us, support us, make us such that we shall love but Thy good pleasure, utter only Thy praise, follow only the pathway of truth, that we may become rich enough to dispense with all save Thee, and receive our gifts from the sea of Thy beneficence, that we may ever strive to exalt Thy Cause and to spread Thy sweet savors far and wide, that we may become oblivious of self and occupied only with Thee, and disown all else and be caught up in Thee.

O Thou Provider, O Thou Forgiver! Grant us Thy grace and loving-kindness, Thy gifts and Thy bestowals, and sustain us, that we may attain our goal. Thou art the Powerful, the Able, the Knower, the Seer; and, verily, Thou art the Generous, and, verily, Thou art the All-Merciful, and, verily, Thou art the Ever-Forgiving, He to Whom repentance is due, He Who forgiveth even the most grievous of sins.   8

O Lord, my God and my Haven in my distress! My Shield and my Shelter in my woes! My Asylum and Refuge in time of need and in my loneliness my Companion! In my anguish my Solace, and in my solitude a loving Friend! The Remover of the pangs of my sorrows and the Pardoner of my sins!

Wholly unto Thee do I turn, fervently imploring Thee with all my heart, my mind and my tongue, to shield me from all that runs counter to Thy will in this, the cycle of Thy divine unity, and to cleanse me of all defilement that will hinder me from seeking, stainless and unsullied, the shade of the tree of Thy grace.

Have mercy, O Lord, on the feeble, make whole the sick, and quench the burning thirst.

Gladden the bosom wherein the fire of Thy love doth smolder, and set it aglow with the flame of Thy celestial love and spirit.

Robe the tabernacles of divine unity with the vesture of holiness, and set upon my head the crown of Thy favor.

Illumine my face with the radiance of the orb of Thy bounty, and graciously aid me in ministering at Thy holy threshold.

Make my heart overflow with love for Thy creatures and grant that I may become the sign of Thy mercy, the token of Thy grace, the promoter of concord amongst Thy loved ones, devoted unto Thee, uttering Thy commemoration and forgetful of self but ever mindful of what is Thine.

O God, my God! Stay not from me the gentle gales of Thy pardon and grace, and deprive me not of the wellsprings of Thine aid and favor.

'Neath the shade of Thy protecting wings let me nestle, and cast upon me the glance of Thine all-protecting eye.

Loose my tongue to laud Thy name amidst Thy people, that my voice may be raised in great assemblies and from my lips may stream the flood of Thy praise.

Thou art, in all truth, the Gracious, the Glorified, the Mighty, the Omnipotent.   9

Home

MEDITATION

Know thou of a certainty that every house wherein the anthem of praise is raised to the Realm of Glory in celebration of the Name of God is indeed a heavenly home, and one of the gardens of delight in the Paradise of God. **1**

PRAYER

Blessed is the spot, and the house, and the place, and the city, and the heart, and the mountain, and the refuge, and the cave, and the valley, and the land, and the sea, and the island, and the meadow where mention of God hath been made, and His praise glorified. 2

Hope

MEDITATIONS

Never lose thy trust in God. Be thou ever hopeful, for the bounties of God never cease to flow upon man. If viewed from one perspective they seem to decrease, but from another they are full and complete. Man is under all conditions immersed in a sea of God's blessings. Therefore, be thou not hopeless under any circumstances, but rather be firm in thy hope. 1

When our thoughts are filled with the bitterness of this world, let us turn our eyes to the sweetness of God's compassion and He will send us heavenly calm! If we are imprisoned in the material world, our spirit can soar into the Heavens and we shall be free indeed! 2

PRAYERS

From the sweet-scented streams of Thine eternity give me to drink, O my God, and of the fruits of the tree of Thy being enable me to taste, O my Hope! From the crystal springs of Thy love suffer me to quaff, O my Glory, and beneath the shadow of Thine everlasting providence let me abide, O my Light! Within the meadows of Thy nearness, before Thy presence, make me able to roam, O my Beloved, and at the right hand of the throne of Thy mercy, seat me, O my Desire! From the fragrant breezes of Thy joy let a breath pass over me, O my Goal, and into the heights of the paradise of Thy reality let me gain admission, O my Adored One! To the melodies of the dove of Thy oneness suffer me to hearken, O Resplendent One, and through the spirit of Thy power and Thy might quicken me, O my Provider! In the spirit of Thy love keep me steadfast, O my Succorer, and in the path of Thy good pleasure set firm my steps, O my Maker! Within the garden of Thine immortality, before Thy countenance, let me abide for ever, O Thou Who art merciful unto me, and upon the seat of Thy glory stablish me, O Thou Who art my Possessor! To the heaven of Thy loving-kindness lift me up, O my Quickener, and unto the Daystar of Thy guidance lead me, O Thou my Attractor! Before the revelations of Thine invisible spirit summon me to be present, O Thou Who art my Origin and my Highest Wish, and unto the essence of the fragrance of Thy beauty, which Thou wilt manifest, cause me to return, O Thou Who art my God!

Potent art Thou to do what pleaseth Thee. Thou art, verily, the Most Exalted, the All-Glorious, the All-Highest.   3

He is the Compassionate, the All-Bountiful! O God, my God! Thou seest me, Thou knowest me; Thou art my Haven and my Refuge. None have I sought nor any will I seek save Thee; no path have I trodden nor any will I tread but the path of Thy love. In the darksome night of despair, my eye turneth expectant and full of hope to the morn of Thy boundless favor and at the hour of dawn my drooping soul is refreshed and strengthened in remembrance of Thy beauty and perfection. He whom the grace of Thy mercy aideth, though he be but a drop, shall become the boundless ocean, and the merest atom which the outpouring of Thy loving-kindness assisteth, shall shine even as the radiant star.

Shelter under Thy protection, O Thou Spirit of purity, Thou Who art the All-Bountiful Provider, this enthralled, enkindled servant of Thine. Aid him in this world of being to remain steadfast and firm in Thy love and grant that this broken-winged bird attain a refuge and shelter in Thy divine nest that abideth upon the celestial tree.   4

Humanity

MEDITATIONS

God, the Almighty, has created all . . . from the dust of earth. He has fashioned them all from the same elements; they are descended from the same race and live upon the same globe. He has created them to dwell beneath the one heaven. As members of the human family and His children He has endowed them with equal susceptibilities. He maintains, protects and is kind to all. He has made no distinction in mercies and graces among His children.   1

Humanity is one kind, one race and progeny, inhabiting the same globe. . . . All mankind are the fruits of one tree, flowers of the same garden, waves of one sea.   2

PRAYERS

Glory be to Thee, O God, for Thy manifestation of love to mankind! O Thou Who art our Life and Light, guide Thy servants in Thy way, and make us rich in Thee and free from all save Thee.

O God, teach us Thy Oneness and give us a realization of Thy Unity, that we may see no one save Thee. Thou art the Merciful and the Giver of bounty!

O God, create in the hearts of Thy beloved the fire of Thy love, that it may consume the thought of everything save Thee.

Reveal to us, O God, Thine exalted eternity— that Thou hast ever been and wilt ever be, and that there is no God save Thee. Verily, in Thee will we find comfort and strength.   3

O Lord! Enable all the peoples of the earth to gain admittance into the Paradise of Thy Faith, so that no created being may remain beyond the bounds of Thy good-pleasure.

From time immemorial Thou hast been potent to do what pleaseth Thee and transcendent above whatsoever Thou desirest.   4

O Thou compassionate Lord, Thou Who art generous and able! We are servants of Thine sheltered beneath Thy providence. Cast Thy glance of favor upon us. Give light to our eyes, hearing to our ears, and understanding and love to our hearts. Render our souls joyous and happy through Thy glad tidings. O Lord! Point out to us the pathway of Thy kingdom and resuscitate all of us through the breaths of the Holy Spirit. Bestow upon us life everlasting and confer upon us never-ending honor. Unify mankind and illumine the world of humanity. May we all follow Thy pathway, long for Thy good pleasure and seek the mysteries of Thy kingdom. O God! Unite us and connect our hearts with Thy indissoluble bond. Verily, Thou art the Giver, Thou art the Kind One and Thou art the Almighty.   5

O Thou kind Lord! O Thou Who art generous and merciful! We are the servants of Thy threshold and are gathered beneath the sheltering shadow of Thy divine unity. The sun of Thy mercy is shining upon all, and the clouds of Thy bounty shower upon all. Thy gifts encompass all, Thy loving providence sustains all, Thy protection overshadows all, and the glances of Thy favor are cast upon all. O Lord! Grant Thine infinite bestowals, and let the light of Thy guidance shine. Illumine the eyes, gladden the hearts with abiding joy. Confer a new spirit upon all people and bestow upon them eternal life. Unlock the gates of true understanding and let the light of faith shine resplendent. Gather all people beneath the shadow of Thy bounty and cause them to unite in harmony, so that they may become as the rays of one sun, as the waves of one ocean, and as the fruit of one tree. May they drink from the same fountain. May they be refreshed by the same breeze. May they receive illumination from the same source of light. Thou art the Giver, the Merciful, the Omnipotent.   6

O holy Lord! O Lord of loving-kindness! We stray about Thy dwelling, longing to behold Thy beauty, and loving all Thy ways. We are hapless, lowly, and of small account. We are paupers: show us mercy, give us bounty; look not upon our failings, hide Thou our endless sins. Whatever we are, still are we Thine, and what we speak and hear is praise of Thee, and it is Thy face we seek, Thy path we follow. Thou art the Lord of loving-kindness, we are sinners and astray and far from home. Wherefore, O Cloud of

Mercy, grant us some drops of rain. O Flowering Bed of grace, send forth a fragrant breeze. O Sea of all bestowals, roll towards us a great wave. O Sun of Bounty, send down a shaft of light. Grant us pity, grant us grace. By Thy beauty, we come with no provision but our sins, with no good deeds to tell of, only hopes. Unless Thy concealing veil doth cover us, and Thy protection shield and cradle us, what power have these helpless souls to rise and serve Thee, what substance have these wretched ones to make a brave display? Thou Who art the Mighty, the All-Powerful, help us, favor us; withered as we are, revive us with showers from Thy clouds of grace; lowly as we are, illumine us with bright rays from the Day-Star of Thy oneness. Cast Thou these thirsty fish into the ocean of Thy mercy, guide Thou this lost caravan to the shelter of Thy singleness; to the wellspring of guidance lead Thou the ones who have wandered far astray, and grant to those who have missed the path a haven within the precincts of Thy might. Lift Thou to these parched lips the bounteous and soft-flowing waters of heaven, raise up these dead to everlasting life. Grant Thou to the blind eyes that will see. Make Thou the deaf to hear, the dumb to speak.

Set Thou the dispirited ablaze, make Thou the heedless mindful, warn Thou the proud, awaken those who sleep.

Thou art the Mighty, Thou art the Bestower, Thou art the Loving. Verily Thou art the Beneficent, the Most Exalted.   7

Humility

MEDITATIONS

Humility exalteth man to the heaven of glory and power, whilst pride abaseth him to the depths of wretchedness and degradation.　　　　1

Every man of discernment, while walking upon the earth, feeleth indeed abashed, inasmuch as he is fully aware that the thing which is the source of his prosperity, his wealth, his might, his exaltation, his advancement and power is, as ordained by God, the very earth which is trodden beneath the feet of all men. There can be no doubt that whoever is cognizant of this truth, is cleansed and sanctified from all pride, arrogance, and vainglory.　　　　2

Every human creature is the servant of God. All have been created and reared by the power and favor of God; all have been blessed with the bounties of the same Sun of divine truth; all have quaffed from the fountain of the infinite mercy of God; and all in His estimation and love are equal as ser-

vants. He is beneficent and kind to all. Therefore, no one should glorify himself over another; no one should manifest pride or superiority toward another; no one should look upon another with scorn and contempt; and no one should deprive or oppress a fellow creature. All must be considered as submerged in the ocean of God's mercy. 3

PRAYERS

I bear witness, O my God, that Thou hast created me to know Thee and to worship Thee. I
testify, at this moment, to my powerlessness and
to Thy might, to my poverty and to Thy wealth.

There is none other God but Thee, the Help
in Peril, the Self-Subsisting.   **4**

Glorified art Thou, O Lord my God! Every
time I venture to make mention of Thee, I
am held back by my mighty sins and grievous
trespasses against Thee, and find myself wholly
deprived of Thy grace, and utterly powerless to
celebrate Thy praise. My great confidence in Thy
bounty, however, reviveth my hope in Thee, and
my certitude that Thou wilt bountifully deal with
me emboldeneth me to extol Thee, and to ask of
Thee the things Thou dost possess.

I implore Thee, O my God, by Thy mercy
that hath surpassed all created things, and to
which all that are immersed beneath the oceans
of Thy names bear witness, not to abandon me
unto my self, for my heart is prone to evil. Guard
me, then, within the stronghold of Thy protec-

tion and the shelter of Thy care. I am he, O my
God, whose only wish is what Thou hast deter-
mined by the power of Thy might. All I have
chosen for myself is to be assisted by Thy gracious appointments and the ruling of Thy will,
and to be aided with the tokens of Thy decree
and judgment.

I beseech Thee, O Thou Who art the Beloved
of the hearts which long for Thee, by the Manifestations of Thy Cause and the Daysprings of
Thine inspiration, and the Exponents of Thy
majesty, and the Treasuries of Thy knowledge,
not to suffer me to be deprived of Thy holy Habitation, Thy Fane and Thy Tabernacle. Aid me,
O my Lord, to attain His hallowed court, and to
circle round His person, and to stand humbly at
His door.

Thou art He Whose power is from everlasting
to everlasting. Nothing escapeth Thy knowledge.
Thou art, verily, the God of power, the God of
glory and wisdom.

Praised be God, the Lord of the worlds!   5

Vouchsafe unto me, O my God, the full measure of Thy love and Thy good-pleasure,
and through the attractions of Thy resplendent

light enrapture our hearts, O Thou Who art the Supreme Evidence and the All-Glorified. Send down upon me, as a token of Thy grace, Thy vitalizing breezes, throughout the daytime and in the night season, O Lord of bounty.

No deed have I done, O my God, to merit beholding Thy face, and I know of a certainty that were I to live as long as the world lasts I would fail to accomplish any deed such as to deserve this favor, inasmuch as the station of a servant shall ever fall short of access to Thy holy precincts, unless Thy bounty should reach me and Thy tender mercy pervade me and Thy loving-kindness encompass me.

All praise be unto Thee, O Thou besides Whom there is none other God. Graciously enable me to ascend unto Thee, to be granted the honor of dwelling in Thy nearness and to have communion with Thee alone. No God is there but Thee.

Indeed shouldst Thou desire to confer blessing upon a servant Thou wouldst blot out from the realm of his heart every mention or disposition except Thine Own mention; and shouldst Thou ordain evil for a servant by reason of that which his hands have unjustly wrought before

Thy face, Thou wouldst test him with the benefits of this world and of the next that he might become preoccupied therewith and forget Thy remembrance.   6

Loved Ones

MEDITATIONS

When you love a member of your family or a compatriot, let it be with a ray of the Infinite Love! Let it be in God, and for God! Wherever you find the attributes of God love that person, whether he be of your family or of another.   1

There are imperfections in every human being, and you will always become unhappy if ye look toward the people themselves. But if you look toward God, you will love them and be kind to them, for the world of God is the world of perfection and complete mercy. Therefore, do not look at the shortcomings of anybody; see with the sight of forgiveness. The imperfect eye beholds imperfections. The eye that covers faults looks toward the Creator of souls. He created them, trains and provides for them, endows them with capacity and life, sight and hearing; therefore, they are the signs of His grandeur. You must love and be kind to everybody, care for the poor, protect the weak, heal the sick, teach and educate the ignorant.   2

PRAYERS

I give thanks to Thee, O my God, that Thou hast suffered me to remember Thee. What else but remembrance of Thee can give delight to my soul or gladness to my heart? Communion with Thee enableth me to dispense with the remembrance of all Thy creatures, and my love for Thee empowereth me to endure the harm which my oppressors inflict upon me.

Send, therefore, unto my loved ones, O my God, what will cheer their hearts, and illumine their faces, and delight their souls. Thou knowest, O my Lord, that their joy is to behold the exaltation of Thy Cause and the glorification of Thy word. Do Thou unveil, therefore, O my God, what will gladden their eyes, and ordain for them the good of this world and of the world which is to come.

Thou art, verily, the God of power, of strength and of bounty.   **3**

Praised be Thou, O Lord my God! Every time I attempt to make mention of Thee, I am hindered by the sublimity of Thy station and the overpowering greatness of Thy might. For were I to praise Thee throughout the length of Thy dominion and the duration of Thy sovereignty, I would find that my praise of Thee can befit only such as are like unto me, who are themselves Thy creatures, and who have been generated through the power of Thy decree and been fashioned through the potency of Thy will. And at whatever time my pen ascribeth glory to any one of Thy names, methinks I can hear the voice of its lamentation in its remoteness from Thee, and can recognize its cry because of its separation from Thy Self. I testify that everything other than Thee is but Thy creation and is held in the hollow of Thy hand. To have accepted any act or praise from Thy creatures is but an evidence of the wonders of Thy grace and bountiful favors, and a manifestation of Thy generosity and providence.

I entreat Thee, O my Lord, by Thy Most Great Name whereby Thou didst separate light from fire, and truth from denial, to send down upon me and upon such of my loved ones as are in my company the good of this world and of the next. Supply us, then, with Thy wondrous gifts that are hid from the eyes of men. Thou art, verily, the Fashioner of all creation. No God is there but Thee, the Almighty, the All-Glorious, the Most High. 4

I beg Thy forgiveness, O my God, and implore pardon after the manner Thou wishest Thy servants to direct themselves to Thee. I beg of Thee to wash away our sins as befitteth Thy Lordship, and to forgive me, my parents, and those who in Thy estimation have entered the abode of Thy love in a manner which is worthy of Thy transcendent sovereignty and well beseemeth the glory of Thy celestial power.

O my God! Thou hast inspired my soul to offer its supplication to Thee, and but for Thee, I would not call upon Thee. Lauded and glorified art Thou; I yield Thee praise inasmuch as Thou didst reveal Thyself unto me, and I beg Thee to forgive me, since I have fallen short in my duty to know Thee and have failed to walk in the path of Thy love. 5

O God, my God! This Thy handmaid is calling upon Thee, trusting in Thee, turning her face unto Thee, imploring Thee to shed Thy heavenly bounties upon her, and to disclose unto her Thy spiritual mysteries, and to cast upon her the lights of Thy Godhead.

O my Lord! Make the eyes of my husband to see. Rejoice Thou his heart with the light of the knowledge of Thee, draw Thou his mind unto Thy luminous beauty, cheer Thou his spirit by revealing unto him Thy manifest splendors.

O my Lord! Lift Thou the veil from before his sight. Rain down Thy plenteous bounties upon him, intoxicate him with the wine of love for Thee, make him one of Thy angels whose feet walk upon this earth even as their souls are soaring through the high heavens. Cause him to become a brilliant lamp, shining out with the light of Thy wisdom in the midst of Thy people.

Verily, Thou art the Precious, the Ever-Bestowing, the Open of Hand.   6

Marriage

MEDITATION

The Lord, peerless is He, hath made woman and man to abide with each other in the closest companionship, and to be even as a single soul. They are two helpmates, two intimate friends, who should be concerned about the welfare of each other.

If they live thus, they will pass through this world with perfect contentment, bliss, and peace of heart, and become the object of divine grace and favor in the Kingdom of heaven. 1

PRAYERS

He is God!
O peerless Lord! In Thine almighty wisdom Thou hast enjoined marriage upon the peoples, that the generations of men may succeed one another in this contingent world, and that ever, so long as the world shall last, they may busy themselves at the Threshold of Thy oneness with servitude and worship, with salutation, adoration and praise. "I have not created spirits and men, but that they should worship me."* Wherefore, wed Thou in the heaven of Thy mercy these two birds of the nest of Thy love, and make them the means of attracting perpetual grace; that from the union of these two seas of love a wave of tenderness may surge and cast the pearls of pure and goodly issue on the shore of life. "He hath let loose the two seas, that they meet each other: Between them is a barrier which they overpass not. Which then of the bounties of your Lord will ye deny? From each He bringeth up greater and lesser pearls."*

---

* Koran 51:56.
* Koran 55:19–22.

O Thou kind Lord! Make Thou this marriage to bring forth coral and pearls. Thou art verily the All-Powerful, the Most Great, the Ever-Forgiving.   2

Glory be unto Thee, O my God! Verily, this Thy servant and this Thy maidservant have gathered under the shadow of Thy mercy and they are united through Thy favor and generosity. O Lord! Assist them in this Thy world and Thy kingdom and destine for them every good through Thy bounty and grace. O Lord! Confirm them in Thy servitude and assist them in Thy service. Suffer them to become the signs of Thy Name in Thy world and protect them through Thy bestowals which are inexhaustible in this world and the world to come. O Lord! They are supplicating the kingdom of Thy mercifulness and invoking the realm of Thy singleness. Verily, they are married in obedience to Thy command. Cause them to become the signs of harmony and unity until the end of time. Verily, Thou art the Omnipotent, the Omnipresent and the Almighty!   3

Material Needs

MEDITATION

Should a man wish to adorn himself with the ornaments of the earth, to wear its apparels, or partake of the benefits it can bestow, no harm can befall him, if he alloweth nothing whatever to intervene between him and God, for God hath ordained every good thing, whether created in the heavens or in the earth, for such of His servants as truly believe in Him. Eat ye, O people, of the good things which God hath allowed you, and deprive not yourselves from His wondrous bounties. Render thanks and praise unto Him, and be of them that are truly thankful. 1

PRAYERS

Dispel my grief by Thy bounty and Thy generosity, O God, my God, and banish mine anguish through Thy sovereignty and Thy might. Thou seest me, O my God, with my face set towards Thee at a time when sorrows have compassed me on every side. I implore Thee, O Thou Who art the Lord of all being, and overshadowest all things visible and invisible, by Thy Name whereby Thou hast subdued the hearts and the souls of men, and by the billows of the Ocean of Thy mercy and the splendors of the Daystar of Thy bounty, to number me with them whom nothing whatsoever hath deterred from setting their faces toward Thee, O Thou Lord of all names and Maker of the heavens!

Thou beholdest, O my Lord, the things which have befallen me in Thy days. I entreat Thee, by Him Who is the Dayspring of Thy names and the Dawning-Place of Thine attributes, to ordain for me what will enable me to arise to serve Thee and to extol Thy virtues. Thou art, verily, the Almighty, the Most Powerful, Who art wont to answer the prayers of all men!

And, finally, I beg of Thee by the light of Thy countenance to bless my affairs, and redeem my debts, and satisfy my needs. Thou art He to Whose power and to Whose dominion every tongue hath testified, and Whose majesty and Whose sovereignty every understanding heart hath acknowledged. No God is there but Thee, Who hearest and art ready to answer.   2

O God, my God! Illumine the brows of Thy true lovers, and support them with angelic hosts of certain triumph. Set firm their feet on Thy straight path, and out of Thine ancient bounty open before them the portals of Thy blessings; for they are expending on Thy pathway what Thou hast bestowed upon them, safeguarding Thy Faith, putting their trust in their remembrance of Thee, offering up their hearts for love of Thee, and withholding not what they possess in adoration for Thy Beauty and in their search for ways to please Thee.

O my Lord! Ordain for them a plenteous share, a destined recompense and sure reward.

Verily, Thou art the Sustainer, the Helper, the Generous, the Bountiful, the Ever-Bestowing.   3

Lord! Pitiful are we, grant us Thy favor; poor, bestow upon us a share from the ocean of Thy wealth; needy, do Thou satisfy us; abased, give us Thy glory. The fowls of the air and the beasts of the field receive their meat each day from Thee, and all beings partake of Thy care and loving-kindness.

Deprive not this feeble one of Thy wondrous grace and vouchsafe by Thy might unto this helpless soul Thy bounty.

Give us our daily bread, and grant Thine increase in the necessities of life, that we may be dependent on none other but Thee, may commune wholly with Thee, may walk in Thy ways and declare Thy mysteries. Thou art the Almighty and the Loving and the Provider of all mankind.   4

Meetings and Gatherings

MEDITATION

Whensoever a company of people shall gather in a meeting place, shall engage in glorifying God, and shall speak with one another of the mysteries of God, beyond any doubt the breathings of the Holy Spirit will blow gently over them, and each shall receive a share thereof.　　　　　**1**

PRAYERS

O God, my God! These are Thy feeble servants; they are Thy loyal bondsmen and Thy handmaidens, who have bowed themselves down before Thine exalted Utterance and humbled themselves at Thy Threshold of light, and borne witness to Thy oneness through which the Sun hath been made to shine in midday splendor. They have listened to the summons Thou didst raise from out Thy hidden Realm, and with hearts quivering with love and rapture, they have responded to Thy call.

O Lord, shower upon them all the outpourings of Thy mercy, rain down upon them all the waters of Thy grace. Make them to grow as beauteous plants in the garden of heaven, and from the full and brimming clouds of Thy bestowals and out of the deep pools of Thine abounding grace make Thou this garden to flower, and keep it ever green and lustrous, ever fresh and shimmering and fair.

Thou art, verily, the Mighty, the Exalted, the Powerful, He Who alone, in the heavens and on the earth, abideth unchanged. There is none other God save Thee, the Lord of manifest tokens and signs. 2

He is God!
O God, my God! These are servants attracted in Thy days by the fragrances of Thy holiness, enkindled with the flame burning in Thy holy tree, responding to Thy voice, uttering Thy praise, awakened by Thy breeze, stirred by Thy sweet savors, beholding Thy signs, understanding Thy verses, hearkening to Thy words, believing Thy Revelation and assured of Thy loving-kindness. Their eyes, O Lord, are fixed upon Thy kingdom of effulgent glory and their faces turned toward Thy dominion on high, their hearts beating with the love of Thy radiant and glorious beauty, their souls consumed with the flame of Thy love, O Lord of this world and the world hereafter, their lives seething with the ardor of their longing for Thee, and their tears poured forth for Thy sake.

Shield them within the stronghold of Thy protection and safety, preserve them in Thy watchful care, look upon them with the eyes of Thy providence and mercy, make them the signs of Thy divine unity that are manifest throughout all regions, the standards of Thy might that wave above Thy mansions of grandeur, the shining lamps that burn with the oil of Thy wisdom in the globes of Thy guidance, the birds of the garden of Thy knowledge that warble upon the topmost boughs in Thy sheltering paradise, and the leviathans of the ocean of Thy bounty that plunge by Thy supreme mercy in the fathomless deeps.

O Lord, my God! Lowly are these servants of Thine, exalt them in Thy kingdom on high; feeble, strengthen them by Thy supreme power; abased, bestow upon them Thy glory in Thine all-highest realm; poor, enrich them in Thy great dominion. Do Thou then ordain for them all the good Thou hast destined in Thy worlds, visible and invisible, prosper them in this world below, gladden their hearts with Thine inspiration, O Lord of all beings! Illumine their hearts with Thy joyful tidings diffused from Thine all-glorious Station, make firm their steps in Thy Most Great Covenant and strengthen their loins in Thy firm Testament, by Thy bounty and promised grace, O Gracious and Merciful One! Thou art, verily, the Gracious, the All-Bountiful.   3

O Thou forgiving Lord! Thou art the shelter of all these Thy servants. Thou knowest the secrets and art aware of all things. We are all helpless, and Thou art the Mighty, the Omnipotent. We are all sinners, and Thou art the Forgiver of sins, the Merciful, the Compassionate.

O Lord! Look not at our shortcomings. Deal with us according to Thy grace and bounty. Our shortcomings are many, but the ocean of Thy forgiveness is boundless. Our weakness is grievous, but the evidences of Thine aid and assistance are clear. Therefore, confirm and strengthen us. Enable us to do that which is worthy of Thy holy Threshold. Illumine our hearts, grant us discerning eyes and attentive ears. Resuscitate the dead and heal the sick. Bestow wealth upon the poor and give peace and security to the fearful. Accept us in Thy kingdom and illumine us with the light of guidance. Thou art the Powerful and the Omnipotent. Thou art the Generous. Thou art the Clement. Thou art the Kind.   **4**

O Thou merciful God! O Thou Who art mighty and powerful! O Thou most kind Father! These servants have gathered together, turning to Thee, supplicating Thy threshold, desiring Thine endless bounties from Thy great assurance. They have no purpose save Thy good pleasure. They have no intention save service to the world of humanity.

O God! Make this assemblage radiant. Make the hearts merciful. Confer the bounties of the Holy Spirit. Endow them with a power from heaven. Bless them with heavenly minds. Increase their sincerity, so that with all humility and contrition they may turn to Thy kingdom and be occupied with service to the world of humanity. May each one become a radiant candle. May each one become a brilliant star. May each one become beautiful in color and redolent of fragrance in the kingdom of God.

O kind Father! Confer Thy blessings. Consider not our shortcomings. Shelter us under Thy protection. Remember not our sins. Heal us with Thy mercy. We are weak; Thou art mighty. We are poor; Thou art rich. We are sick; Thou art the Physician. We are needy; Thou art most generous.

O God! Endow us with Thy providence. Thou art the Powerful. Thou art the Giver. Thou art the Beneficent.   5

O Thou kind Lord! These are Thy servants who have gathered in this meeting, have turned unto Thy kingdom and are in need of Thy bestowal and blessing. O Thou God! Manifest and make evident the signs of Thy oneness which have been deposited in all the realities of life. Reveal and unfold the virtues which Thou hast made latent and concealed in these human realities.

O God! We are as plants, and Thy bounty is as the rain; refresh and cause these plants to grow through Thy bestowal. We are Thy servants; free us from the fetters of material existence. We are ignorant; make us wise. We are dead; make us alive. We are material; endow us with spirit. We are deprived; make us the intimates of Thy mysteries. We are needy; enrich and bless us from Thy boundless treasury. O God! Resuscitate us; give us sight; give us hearing; familiarize us with the mysteries of life, so that the secrets of Thy kingdom may become revealed to us in this world of existence and we may confess Thy oneness. Every bestowal emanates from Thee; every benediction is Thine.

Thou art mighty. Thou art powerful. Thou art the Giver, and Thou art the Ever-Bounteous.   6

O my God! O my God! Verily, these servants are turning to Thee, supplicating Thy kingdom of mercy. Verily, they are attracted by Thy holiness and set aglow with the fire of Thy love, seeking confirmation from Thy wondrous kingdom, and hoping for attainment in Thy heavenly realm. Verily, they long for the descent of Thy bestowal, desiring illumination from the Sun of Reality. O Lord! Make them radiant lamps, merciful signs, fruitful trees and shining stars. May they come forth in Thy service and be connected with Thee by the bonds and ties of Thy love, longing for the lights of Thy favor. O Lord! Make them signs of guidance, standards of Thine immortal kingdom, waves of the sea of Thy mercy, mirrors of the light of Thy majesty.

Verily, Thou art the Generous. Verily, Thou art the Merciful. Verily, Thou art the Precious, the Beloved. 7

Morning

MEDITATIONS

Reflect, O people, on the grace and blessings of your Lord, and yield Him thanks at eventide and dawn.   1

Let each morn be better than its eve and each morrow richer than its yesterday.   2

Engage ye in the remembrance of God at dawn; rise ye up to praise and glorify Him.   3

PRAYERS

I have wakened in Thy shelter, O my God, and it becometh him that seeketh that shelter to abide within the Sanctuary of Thy protection and the Stronghold of Thy defense. Illumine my inner being, O my Lord, with the splendors of the Dayspring of Thy Revelation, even as Thou didst illumine my outer being with the morning light of Thy favor.   4

I have risen this morning by Thy grace, O my God, and left my home trusting wholly in Thee, and committing myself to Thy care. Send down, then, upon me, out of the heaven of Thy mercy, a blessing from Thy side, and enable me to return home in safety even as Thou didst enable me to set out under thy protection with my thoughts fixed steadfastly upon Thee.

There is none other God but Thee, the One, the Incomparable, the All-Knowing, the All-Wise.   5

Nearness to God

MEDITATIONS

The essence of love is for man to turn his heart to the Beloved One, and sever himself from all else but Him, and desire naught save that which is the desire of his Lord. 1

Bahá'u'lláh proclaims . . . that God inspires His servants and is revealed through them. He says, "Thy heart is My home; sanctify it for My descent. Thy spirit is My place of revelation; cleanse it for My manifestation." Therefore, we learn that nearness to God is possible through devotion to Him, through entrance into the Kingdom and service to humanity; it is attained by unity with mankind and through loving-kindness to all; it is dependent upon investigation of truth, acquisition of praiseworthy virtues, service in the cause of universal peace and personal sanctification. In a word, nearness to God necessitates sacrifice of self, severance and the giving up of all to Him. Nearness is likeness. 2

Prayers

O my Lord! Make Thy beauty to be my food, and Thy presence my drink, and Thy pleasure my hope, and praise of Thee my action, and remembrance of Thee my companion, and the power of Thy sovereignty my succorer, and Thy habitation my home, and my dwelling-place the seat Thou hast sanctified from the limitations imposed upon them who are shut out as by a veil from Thee.

Thou art, verily, the Almighty, the All-Glorious, the Most Powerful.   3

O God, my God! I have turned in repentance unto Thee, and verily Thou art the Pardoner, the Compassionate.

O God, my God! I have returned to Thee, and verily Thou art the Ever-Forgiving, the Gracious.

O God, my God! I have clung to the cord of Thy bounty, and with Thee is the storehouse of all that is in heaven and earth.

O God, my God! I have hastened toward Thee, and verily Thou art the Forgiver, the Lord of grace abounding.

O God, my God! I thirst for the celestial wine of Thy grace, and verily Thou art the Giver, the Bountiful, the Gracious, the Almighty.

O God, my God! I testify that Thou hast revealed Thy Cause, fulfilled Thy promise and sent down from the heaven of Thy grace that which hath drawn unto Thee the hearts of Thy favored ones. Well is it with him that hath held fast unto Thy firm cord and clung to the hem of Thy resplendent robe!

I ask Thee, O Lord of all being and King of the seen and unseen, by Thy power, Thy majesty and Thy sovereignty, to grant that my name may be recorded by Thy pen of glory among Thy devoted ones, them whom the scrolls of the sinful hindered not from turning to the light of Thy countenance, O prayer-hearing, prayer-answering God!   4

Lauded be Thy name, O my God and the God of all things, my Glory and the Glory of all things, my Desire and the Desire of all things, my Strength and the Strength of all things, my King and the King of all things, my Possessor and the Possessor of all things, my Aim and the Aim of all things, my Mover and the Mover of all things! Suffer me not, I implore Thee, to be kept back from the ocean of Thy tender mercies, nor to be far removed from the shores of nearness to Thee.

Aught else except Thee, O my Lord, profiteth me not, and near access to anyone save Thyself availeth me nothing. I entreat Thee by the plenteousness of Thy riches, whereby Thou didst dispense with all else except Thyself, to number me with such as have set their faces towards Thee, and arisen to serve Thee.

Forgive, then, O my Lord, Thy servants and Thy handmaidens. Thou, truly, art the Ever-Forgiving, the Most Compassionate.   5

I know not, O my God, what the Fire is which Thou didst kindle in Thy land. Earth can never cloud its splendor, nor water quench its flame. All the peoples of the world are powerless to resist its force. Great is the blessedness of him that hath drawn nigh unto it, and heard its roaring.

Some, O my God, Thou didst, through Thy strengthening grace, enable to approach it, while others Thou didst keep back by reason of what their hands have wrought in Thy days. Whoso hath hasted towards it and attained unto it hath, in his eagerness to gaze on Thy beauty, yielded his life in Thy path, and ascended unto Thee, wholly detached from aught else except Thyself.

I beseech Thee, O my Lord, by this Fire which blazeth and rageth in the world of creation, to rend asunder the veils that have hindered me from appearing before the throne of Thy majesty, and from standing at the door of Thy gate. Do Thou ordain for me, O my Lord, every good thing Thou didst send down in Thy Book, and suffer me not to be far removed from the shelter of Thy mercy.

Powerful art Thou to do what pleaseth Thee. Thou art, verily, the All-Powerful, the Most Generous.   6

Suffer me, O my God, to draw nigh unto Thee, and to abide within the precincts of Thy court, for remoteness from Thee hath well-nigh consumed me. Cause me to rest under the shadow of the wings of Thy grace, for the flame of my separation from Thee hath melted my heart within me. Draw me nearer unto the river that is life indeed, for my soul burneth with thirst in its ceaseless search after Thee. My sighs, O my God, proclaim the bitterness of mine anguish, and the tears I shed attest my love for Thee.

I beseech Thee, by the praise wherewith Thou praisest Thyself and the glory wherewith Thou glorifiest Thine own Essence, to grant that we may be numbered among them that have recognized Thee and acknowledged Thy sovereignty in Thy days. Help us then to quaff, O my God, from the fingers of mercy the living waters of Thy loving-kindness, that we may utterly forget all else except Thee, and be occupied only with Thy Self. Powerful art Thou to do what Thou willest. No God is there beside Thee, the Mighty, the Help in Peril, the Self-Subsisting.

Glorified be Thy name, O Thou Who art the King of all Kings! 7

O my God! O my God! This, Thy servant, hath advanced towards Thee, is passionately wandering in the desert of Thy love, walking in the path of Thy service, anticipating Thy favors, hoping for Thy bounty, relying upon Thy kingdom, and intoxicated by the wine of Thy gift. O my God! Increase the fervor of his affection for Thee, the constancy of his praise of Thee, and the ardor of his love for Thee.

Verily, Thou art the Most Generous, the Lord of grace abounding. There is no other God but Thee, the Forgiving, the Merciful. 8

Praise and Gratitude

MEDITATIONS

Happy the days that have been consecrated to the remembrance of God, and blessed the hours which have been spent in praise of Him Who is the All-Wise.   1

In this day, to thank God for His bounties consisteth in possessing a radiant heart, and a soul open to the promptings of the spirit. This is the essence of thanksgiving.   2

PRAYERS

My God, Whom I worship and adore! I bear witness unto Thy unity and Thy oneness, and acknowledge Thy gifts, both in the past and in the present. Thou art the All-Bountiful, the overflowing showers of Whose mercy have rained down upon high and low alike, and the splendors of Whose grace have been shed over both the obedient and the rebellious.

O God of mercy, before Whose door the quintessence of mercy hath bowed down, and round the sanctuary of Whose Cause loving-kindness, in its inmost spirit, hath circled, we beseech Thee, entreating Thine ancient grace, and seeking Thy present favor, that Thou mayest have mercy upon all who are the manifestations of the world of being, and deny them not the outpourings of Thy grace in Thy days.

All are but poor and needy, and Thou, verily, art the All-Possessing, the All-Subduing, the All-Powerful.   3

Magnified be Thy name, O Lord my God! Thou art He Whom all things worship and Who worshipeth no one, Who is the Lord of all things and is the vassal of none, Who knoweth all things and is known of none. Thou didst wish to make Thyself known unto men; therefore, Thou didst, through a word of Thy mouth, bring creation into being and fashion the universe. There is none other God except Thee, the Fashioner, the Creator, the Almighty, the Most Powerful.

I implore Thee, by this very word that hath shone forth above the horizon of Thy will, to enable me to drink deep of the living waters through which Thou hast vivified the hearts of Thy chosen ones and quickened the souls of them that love Thee, that I may, at all times and under all conditions, turn my face wholly towards Thee.

Thou art the God of power, of glory and bounty. No God is there beside Thee, the Supreme Ruler, the All-Glorious, the Omniscient.   4

In the Name of God, the Most High! Lauded and glorified art Thou, Lord, God Omnipotent! Thou before Whose wisdom the wise falleth short and faileth, before Whose knowledge the learned confesseth his ignorance, before Whose

might the strong waxeth weak, before Whose
wealth the rich testifieth to his poverty, before
Whose light the enlightened is lost in darkness,
toward the shrine of Whose knowledge turneth
the essence of all understanding and around the
sanctuary of Whose presence circle the souls of
all mankind.

How then can I sing and tell of Thine Essence, which the wisdom of the wise and the
learning of the learned have failed to comprehend, inasmuch as no man can sing that which
he understandeth not, nor recount that unto
which he cannot attain, whilst Thou hast been
from everlasting the Inaccessible, the Unsearch-
able. Powerless though I be to rise to the heavens
of Thy glory and soar in the realms of Thy knowledge, I can but recount Thy tokens that tell of
Thy glorious handiwork.

By Thy Glory! O Beloved of all hearts, Thou
that alone canst still the pangs of yearning for
Thee! Though all the dwellers of heaven and earth
unite to glorify the least of Thy signs, wherein
and whereby Thou hast revealed Thyself, yet
would they fail, how much more to praise Thy
holy Word, the creator of all Thy tokens.

All praise and glory be to Thee, Thou of

Whom all things have testified that Thou art one and there is none other God but Thee, Who hast been from everlasting exalted above all peer or likeness and to everlasting shalt remain the same. All kings are but Thy servants and all beings, visible and invisible, as naught before Thee. There is none other God but Thee, the Gracious, the Powerful, the Most High.   5

My God, my Adored One, my King, my Desire! What tongue can voice my thanks to Thee? I was heedless, Thou didst awaken me. I had turned back from Thee, Thou didst graciously aid me to turn towards Thee. I was as one dead, Thou didst quicken me with the water of life. I was withered, Thou didst revive me with the heavenly stream of Thine utterance which hath flowed forth from the Pen of the All-Merciful.

O Divine Providence! All existence is begotten by Thy bounty; deprive it not of the waters of Thy generosity, neither do Thou withhold it from the ocean of Thy mercy. I beseech Thee to aid and assist me at all times and under all conditions, and seek from the heaven of Thy grace Thine ancient favor. Thou art, in truth, the Lord of bounty, and the Sovereign of the kingdom of eternity.   6

All majesty and glory, O my God, and all dominion and light and grandeur and splendor be unto Thee. Thou bestowest sovereignty on whom Thou willest and dost withhold it from whom Thou desirest. No God is there but Thee, the All-Possessing, the Most Exalted. Thou art He Who createth from naught the universe and all that dwell therein. There is nothing worthy of Thee except Thyself, while all else but Thee are as outcasts in Thy holy presence and are as nothing when compared to the glory of Thine Own Being.

Far be it from me to extol Thy virtues save by what Thou hast extolled Thyself in Thy weighty Book where Thou sayest, "No vision taketh in Him, but He taketh in all vision. He is the Subtile, the All-Perceiving."* Glory be unto Thee, O my God, indeed no mind or vision, however keen or discriminating, can ever grasp the nature of the most insignificant of Thy signs. Verily, Thou art

---

* Koran 6:103.

God, no God is there besides Thee. I bear witness that Thou Thyself alone art the sole expression of Thine attributes, that the praise of no
one besides Thee can ever attain to Thy holy court
nor can Thine attributes ever be fathomed by
anyone other than Thyself.

Glory be unto Thee, Thou art exalted above
the description of anyone save Thyself, since it is
beyond human conception to befittingly magnify
Thy virtues or to comprehend the inmost reality
of Thine Essence. Far be it from Thy glory that
Thy creatures should describe Thee or that anyone besides Thyself should ever know Thee. I
have known Thee, O my God, by reason of Thy
making Thyself known unto me, for hadst Thou
not revealed Thyself unto me, I would not have
known Thee. I worship Thee by virtue of Thy
summoning me unto Thee, for had it not been
for Thy summons I would not have worshiped
Thee.   7

Lauded be Thy Name, O Lord our God! Thou
art in truth the Knower of things unseen.
Ordain for us such good as Thine all-embracing
knowledge can measure. Thou art the sovereign
Lord, the Almighty, the Best-Beloved.

All praise be unto Thee, O Lord! We shall seek Thy grace on the appointed Day and shall put our whole reliance in Thee, Who art our Lord. Glorified art Thou, O God! Grant us that which is good and seemly that we may be able to dispense with everything but Thee. Verily, Thou art the Lord of all worlds.

O God! Recompense those who endure patiently in Thy days, and strengthen their hearts to walk undeviatingly in the path of Truth. Grant then, O Lord, such goodly gifts as would enable them to gain admittance into Thy blissful Paradise. Exalted art Thou, O Lord God. Let Thy heavenly blessings descend upon homes whose inmates have believed in Thee. Verily, unsurpassed art Thou in sending down divine blessings. Send forth, O God, such hosts as would render Thy faithful servants victorious. Thou dost fashion the created things through the power of Thy decree as Thou pleasest. Thou art in truth the Sovereign, the Creator, the All-Wise.

Say: God is indeed the Maker of all things. He giveth sustenance in plenty to whomsoever He willeth. He is the Creator, the Source of all beings, the Fashioner, the Almighty, the Maker, the All-Wise. He is the Bearer of the most excellent titles throughout the heavens and the earth and whatever lieth between them. All do His bidding, and all the dwellers of earth and heaven celebrate His praise, and unto Him shall all return.   8

O Thou, my God, Who guidest the seeker to the pathway that leadeth aright, Who deliverest the lost and blinded soul out of the wastes of perdition, Thou Who bestowest upon the sincere great bounties and favors, Who guardest the frightened within Thine impregnable refuge, Who answerest, from Thine all-highest horizon, the cry of those who cry out unto Thee. Praised be Thou, O my Lord! Thou hast guided the distracted out of the death of unbelief, and hast brought those who draw nigh unto Thee to the journey's goal, and hast rejoiced the assured among Thy servants by granting them their most cherished desires, and hast, from Thy Kingdom of beauty, opened before the faces of those who yearn after Thee the gates of reunion, and hast rescued them from the fires of deprivation and loss—so that they hastened unto Thee and gained Thy presence, and arrived at Thy welcoming door, and received of gifts an abundant share.

O my Lord, they thirsted, Thou didst lift to their parched lips the waters of reunion. O Tender One, Bestowing One, Thou didst calm their pain with the balm of Thy bounty and grace, and didst heal their ailments with the sovereign medicine of Thy compassion. O Lord, make firm their feet on Thy straight path, make wide for them the needle's eye, and cause them, dressed in royal robes, to walk in glory for ever and ever.

Verily, art Thou the Generous, the Ever-Giving, the Precious, the Most Bountiful. There is none other God but Thee, the Mighty, the Powerful, the Exalted, the Victorious.   9

Protection

MEDITATIONS

God sufficeth unto me; He is the One Who holdeth in His grasp the kingdom of all things. Through the power of His hosts of heaven and earth and whatever lieth between them, He protecteth whomsoever among His servants He willeth. God, in truth, keepeth watch over all things.　　1

All the kingdoms of heaven and earth and whatever is between them are God's, and His power is supreme over all things. All the treasures of earth and heaven and everything between them are His, and His protection extendeth over all things.　　2

When you call on the Mercy of God waiting to reinforce you, your strength will be tenfold.　　3

PRAYERS

O God, my God! I have set out from my home, holding fast unto the cord of Thy love, and I have committed myself wholly to Thy care and Thy protection. I entreat Thee by Thy power through which Thou didst protect Thy loved ones from the wayward and the perverse, and from every contumacious oppressor, and every wicked doer who hath strayed far from Thee, to keep me safe by Thy bounty and Thy grace. Enable me, then, to return to my home by Thy power and Thy might. Thou art, truly, the Almighty, the Help in Peril, the Self-Subsisting. 4

Praised be Thou, O Lord my God! This is Thy servant who hath quaffed from the hands of Thy grace the wine of Thy tender mercy, and tasted of the savor of Thy love in Thy days. I beseech Thee, by the embodiments of Thy names whom no grief can hinder from rejoicing in Thy love or from gazing on Thy face, and whom all the hosts of the heedless are powerless to cause to turn aside from the path of Thy pleasure, to supply him with the good things Thou dost possess, and to raise him up to such heights that he will regard the world even as a shadow that vanisheth swifter than the twinkling of an eye.

Keep him safe also, O my God, by the power of Thine immeasurable majesty, from all that Thou abhorrest. Thou art, verily, his Lord and the Lord of all worlds.   5

Glorified art Thou, O Lord my God! Every man of insight confesseth Thy sovereignty and Thy dominion, and every discerning eye perceiveth the greatness of Thy majesty and the compelling power of Thy might. The winds of tests are powerless to hold back them that enjoy near access to Thee from setting their faces towards the horizon of Thy glory, and the tempests of trials must fail to draw away and hinder such as are wholly devoted to Thy will from approaching Thy court.

Methinks, the lamp of Thy love is burning in their hearts, and the light of Thy tenderness is lit within their breasts. Adversities are incapable of estranging them from Thy Cause, and the vicissitudes of fortune can never cause them to stray from Thy pleasure.

I beseech Thee, O my God, by them and by
the sighs which their hearts utter in their separation from Thee, to keep them safe from the mischief of Thine adversaries, and to nourish their
souls with what Thou hast ordained for Thy loved
ones on whom shall come no fear and who shall
not be put to grief.   6

I adjure Thee by Thy might, O my God! Let
no harm beset me in times of tests, and in
moments of heedlessness guide my steps aright
through Thine inspiration. Thou art God,
potent art Thou to do what Thou desirest. No one
can withstand Thy Will or thwart Thy Purpose. 7

O my Lord! Thou knowest that the people
are encircled with pain and calamities and
are environed with hardships and trouble. Every
trial doth attack man and every dire adversity
doth assail him like unto the assault of a serpent.
There is no shelter and asylum for him except
under the wing of Thy protection, preservation,
guard and custody.

O Thou the Merciful One! O my Lord! Make
Thy protection my armor, Thy preservation my
shield, humbleness before the door of Thy one-

ness my guard, and Thy custody and defense my fortress and my abode. Preserve me from the suggestions of self and desire, and guard me from every sickness, trial, difficulty and ordeal.

Verily, Thou art the Protector, the Guardian, the Preserver, the Sufficer, and verily, Thou art the Merciful of the Most Merciful.   8

Purity

MEDITATIONS

Wings that are besmirched with mire can never soar.   1

The pure heart is the one that is entirely cut away from self. To be selfless is to be pure.   2

The Teachings which come from God are heavenly outpourings of grace; they are rain-showers of divine mercy, and they cleanse the human heart.
. . . In every aspect of life, purity and holiness, cleanliness and refinement, exalt the human condition and further the development of man's inner reality. Even in the physical realm, cleanliness will conduce to spirituality. . . . And although bodily cleanliness is a physical thing, it hath, nevertheless, a powerful influence on the life of the spirit.   3

PRAYERS

Create in me a pure heart, O my God, and renew a tranquil conscience within me, O my Hope! Through the spirit of power confirm Thou me in Thy Cause, O my Best-Beloved, and by the light of Thy glory reveal unto me Thy path, O Thou the Goal of my desire! Through the power of Thy transcendent might lift me up unto the heaven of Thy holiness, O Source of my being, and by the breezes of Thine eternity gladden me, O Thou Who art my God! Let Thine everlasting melodies breathe tranquillity on me, O my Companion, and let the riches of Thine ancient countenance deliver me from all except Thee, O my Master, and let the tidings of the revelation of Thine incorruptible Essence bring me joy, O Thou Who art the most manifest of the manifest and the most hidden of the hidden! 4

He is God! O God, my God! Bestow upon me a pure heart, like unto a pearl. 5

Sharing God's Love

MEDITATIONS

Follow well the light of truth, in the Holy Teachings, and God will strengthen you by His Holy Spirit so that you will be enabled to overcome the difficulties, and to destroy the prejudices which cause separation and hatred. . . . Let your hearts be filled with the great love of God, let it be felt by all; for every man is a servant of God, and all are entitled to a share of the Divine Bounty. 1

Do not be content with showing friendship in words alone, let your heart burn with loving kindness for all who may cross your path. 2

PRAYERS

O God, Who art the Author of all Manifestations, the Source of all Sources, the Fountainhead of all Revelations, and the Wellspring of all Lights! I testify that by Thy Name the heaven of understanding hath been adorned, and the ocean of utterance hath surged, and the dispensations of Thy providence have been promulgated unto the followers of all religions.

I beseech Thee so to enrich me as to dispense with all save Thee, and be made independent of anyone except Thyself. Rain down, then, upon me out of the clouds of Thy bounty that which shall profit me in every world of Thy worlds. Assist me, then, through Thy strengthening grace, so to serve Thy Cause amidst Thy servants that I may show forth what will cause me to be remembered as long as Thine own kingdom endureth and Thy dominion will last.

This is Thy servant, O my Lord, who with his whole being hath turned unto the horizon of Thy bounty, and the ocean of Thy grace, and the heaven of Thy gifts. Do with me then as becometh Thy majesty, and Thy glory, and Thy bounteousness, and Thy grace.

Thou, in truth, art the God of strength and power, Who art meet to answer them that pray Thee. There is no God save Thee, the All-Knowing, the All-Wise.   3

O Divine Providence! This assemblage is composed of Thy friends who are attracted to Thy beauty and are set ablaze by the fire of Thy love. Turn these souls into heavenly angels, resuscitate them through the breath of Thy Holy Spirit, grant them eloquent tongues and resolute hearts, bestow upon them heavenly power and merciful susceptibilities, cause them to become the promulgators of the oneness of mankind and the cause of love and concord in the world of humanity, so that the perilous darkness of ignorant prejudice may vanish through the light of the Sun of Truth, this dreary world may become illumined, this material realm may absorb the rays of the world of spirit, these different colors may merge into one color and the melody of praise may rise to the kingdom of Thy sanctity.

Verily, Thou art the Omnipotent and the Almighty!   4

O God, my God! Aid Thou Thy trusted servants to have loving and tender hearts. Help them to spread, amongst all the nations of the earth, the light of guidance that cometh from the Company on high. Verily, Thou art the Strong, the Powerful, the Mighty, the All-Subduing, the Ever-Giving. Verily, Thou art the Generous, the Gentle, the Tender, the Most Bountiful.   5

Spiritual Growth

Meditations

Truthfulness is the foundation of all human virtues. Without truthfulness progress and success, in all the worlds of God, are impossible for any soul. When this holy attribute is established in man, all the divine qualities will also be acquired.   1

The troubles of this world pass, and what we have left is what we have made of our souls; so it is to this we must look—to becoming more spiritual, drawing nearer to God, no matter what our human minds and bodies go through.   2

PRAYERS

O my God, the God of bounty and mercy!
Thou art that King by Whose commanding word the whole creation hath been called into
being; and Thou art that All-Bountiful One the
doings of Whose servants have never hindered
Him from showing forth His grace, nor have they
frustrated the revelations of His bounty.

Suffer this servant, I beseech Thee, to attain unto
that which is the cause of his salvation in every world
of Thy worlds. Thou art, verily, the Almighty, the
Most Powerful, the All-Knowing, the All-Wise. **3**

O Thou Whose face is the object of my adoration, Whose beauty is my sanctuary,
Whose habitation is my goal, Whose praise is
my hope, Whose providence is my companion,
Whose love is the cause of my being, Whose
mention is my solace, Whose nearness is my desire, Whose presence is my dearest wish and highest aspiration, I entreat Thee not to withhold from
me the things Thou didst ordain for the chosen
ones among Thy servants. Supply me, then, with
the good of this world and of the next.

Thou, truly, art the King of all men. There is no God but Thee, the Ever-Forgiving, the Most Generous.   4

Glorified art Thou, O Lord my God! I give Thee thanks inasmuch as Thou hast called me into being in Thy days, and infused into me Thy love and Thy knowledge. I beseech Thee, by Thy name whereby the goodly pearls of Thy wisdom and Thine utterance were brought forth out of the treasuries of the hearts of such of Thy servants as are nigh unto Thee, and through which the Daystar of Thy name, the Compassionate, hath shed its radiance upon all that are in Thy heaven and on Thy earth, to supply me, by Thy grace and bounty, with Thy wondrous and hidden bounties.

These are the earliest days of my life, O my God, which Thou hast linked with Thine own days. Now that Thou hast conferred upon me so great an honor, withhold not from me the things Thou hast ordained for Thy chosen ones.

I am, O my God, but a tiny seed which Thou hast sown in the soil of Thy love, and caused to spring forth by the hand of Thy bounty. This seed craveth, therefore, in its inmost being, for the waters of Thy mercy and the living fountain of Thy grace. Send down upon it, from the heaven of Thy loving-kindness, that which will enable it to flourish beneath Thy shadow and within the borders of Thy court. Thou art He Who watereth the hearts of all that have recognized Thee from Thy plenteous stream and the fountain of Thy living waters.

Praised be God, the Lord of the worlds.　　5

O God, my God! Shield Thy trusted servants from the evils of self and passion, protect them with the watchful eye of Thy loving-kindness from all rancor, hate and envy, shelter them in the impregnable stronghold of Thy care and, safe from the darts of doubtfulness, make them the manifestations of Thy glorious signs, illumine their faces with the effulgent rays shed from the Dayspring of Thy divine unity, gladden their hearts with the verses revealed from Thy holy kingdom, strengthen their loins by Thine all-swaying power that cometh from Thy realm of glory. Thou art the All-Bountiful, the Protector, the Almighty, the Gracious.　　6

O Lord, my God! Praise and thanksgiving be unto Thee for Thou hast guided me to the highway of the kingdom, suffered me to walk in this straight and far-stretching path, illumined my eye by beholding the splendors of Thy light, inclined my ear to the melodies of the birds of holiness from the kingdom of mysteries and attracted my heart with Thy love among the righteous.

O Lord! Confirm me with the Holy Spirit, so that I may call in Thy Name amongst the nations and give the glad tidings of the manifestation of Thy kingdom amongst mankind.

O Lord! I am weak, strengthen me with Thy power and potency. My tongue falters, suffer me to utter Thy commemoration and praise. I am lowly, honor me through admitting me into Thy kingdom. I am remote, cause me to approach the threshold of Thy mercifulness. O Lord! Make me a brilliant lamp, a shining star and a blessed tree, adorned with fruit, its branches overshadowing all these regions. Verily, Thou art the Mighty, the Powerful and Unconstrained.   7

O my Lord! O my Lord! This is a lamp lighted by the fire of Thy love and ablaze with the flame which is ignited in the tree of Thy mercy. O my Lord! Increase his enkindlement, heat and

flame, with the fire which is kindled in the Sinai*
of Thy Manifestation. Verily, Thou art the
Confirmer, the Assister, the Powerful, the Generous, the Loving.   8

O my Lord, no words do I find to glorify
Thee; no way do I see for the bird of my
mind to soar upward to Thy Kingdom of Holiness; for Thou, in Thy very essence, art sanctified above those above those tributes, and in Thy
very being art beyond the reach of those praises
which are offered Thee by the people that Thou
hast created. In the sanctity of Thine own being
hast Thou ever been exalted above the understanding of the learned among the Company on
high, and forever wilt Thou remain enwrapped
within the holiness of Thine own reality,
unreached by the knowledge of those dwellers in
Thine exalted Kingdom who glorify Thy Name.

O God, my God! How can I glorify or describe Thee inaccessible as Thou art; immeasurably high and sanctified art Thou above every
description and praise.

---

* The Biblical mountain often associated with Moses
and the revelation of the Ten Commandments.

O God, my God! Have mercy then upon my helpless state, my poverty, my misery, my abasement! Give me to drink from the generous cup of Thy grace and forgiveness, stir me with the sweet scents of Thy love, gladden my bosom with the light of Thy knowledge, purify my soul with the mysteries of Thy oneness, raise me to life with the gentle breeze that cometh from the gardens of Thy mercy—till I sever myself from all else but Thee, and lay hold of the hem of Thy garment of grandeur, and consign to oblivion all that is not Thee, and be companioned by the sweet breathings that waft during these Thy days, and attain unto faithfulness at Thy Threshold of Holiness, and arise to serve Thy Cause, and to be humble before Thy loved ones, and, in the presence of Thy favored ones, to be nothingness itself.

Verily art Thou the Helper, the Sustainer, the Exalted, the Most Generous.   9

Strength

MEDITATIONS

The source of courage and power is the promotion of the Word of God, and steadfastness in His Love.   1

The Almighty will no doubt grant you the help of His grace, will invest you with the tokens of His might, and will endue your souls with the sustaining power of His holy Spirit.   2

Our Heavenly Father will always give us the strength to meet and overcome tests if we turn with all our hearts to Him, and difficulties if they are met in the right spirit only make us rely on God more firmly and completely.   3

PRAYERS

Lauded be Thy Name, O Lord my God! I am Thy servant who hath laid hold on the cord of Thy tender mercies, and clung to the hem of Thy bounteousness. I entreat Thee by Thy name whereby Thou hast subjected all created things, both visible and invisible, and through which the breath that is life indeed was wafted over the entire creation, to strengthen me by Thy power which hath encompassed the heavens and the earth, and to guard me from all sickness and tribulation. I bear witness that Thou art the Lord of all names, and the Ordainer of all that may please Thee. There is none other God but Thee, the Almighty, the All-Knowing, the All-Wise.

Do Thou ordain for me, O my Lord, what will profit me in every world of Thy worlds. Supply me, then, with what Thou hast written down for the chosen ones among Thy creatures, whom neither the blame of the blamer, nor the clamor of the infidel, nor the estrangement of such as have withdrawn from Thee, hath deterred from turning towards Thee.

Thou, truly, art the Help in Peril through the power of Thy sovereignty. No God is there save Thee, the Almighty, the Most Powerful.   **4**

Glorified be Thy name, O Lord my God! I beseech Thee by Thy power that hath encompassed all created things, and by Thy sovereignty that hath transcended the entire creation, and by Thy Word which was hidden in Thy wisdom and whereby Thou didst create Thy heaven and Thy earth, both to enable us to be steadfast in our love for Thee and in our obedience to Thy pleasure, and to fix our gaze upon Thy face, and celebrate Thy glory. Empower us, then, O my God, to spread abroad Thy signs among Thy creatures, and to guard Thy Faith in Thy realm. Thou hast ever existed independently of the mention of any of Thy creatures, and wilt remain as Thou hast been for ever and ever.

In Thee I have placed my whole confidence, unto Thee I have turned my face, to the cord of Thy loving providence I have clung, and towards the shadow of Thy mercy I have hastened. Cast me not as one disappointed out of Thy door, O my God, and withhold not from me Thy grace, for Thee alone do I seek. No God is there beside Thee, the Ever-Forgiving, the Most Bountiful.

Praise be to Thee, O Thou Who art the Beloved of them that have known Thee!   5

Unity

It is not for him to pride himself who loveth his own country, but rather for him who loveth the whole world. The earth is but one country, and mankind its citizens. 1

The fundamental purpose animating the Faith of God and His Religion is to safeguard the interests and promote the unity of the human race, and to foster the spirit of love and fellowship amongst men. Suffer it not to become a source of dissension and discord, of hate and enmity. 2

PRAYERS

O my God! O my God! Unite the hearts of Thy servants, and reveal to them Thy great purpose. May they follow Thy commandments and abide in Thy law. Help them, O God, in their endeavor, and grant them strength to serve Thee. O God! Leave them not to themselves, but guide their steps by the light of Thy knowledge, and cheer their hearts by Thy love. Verily, Thou art their Helper and their Lord.   3

O Thou kind Lord! Thou hast created all humanity from the same stock. Thou hast decreed that all shall belong to the same household. In Thy Holy Presence they are all Thy servants, and all mankind are sheltered beneath Thy Tabernacle; all have gathered together at Thy Table of Bounty; all are illumined through the light of Thy Providence.

O God! Thou art kind to all, Thou hast provided for all, dost shelter all, conferrest life upon all. Thou hast endowed each and all with talents and faculties, and all are submerged in the Ocean of Thy Mercy.

O Thou kind Lord! Unite all. Let the religions agree and make the nations one, so that they may see each other as one family and the whole earth as one home. May they all live together in perfect harmony.

O God! Raise aloft the banner of the oneness of mankind.

O God! Establish the Most Great Peace.

Cement Thou, O God, the hearts together.

O Thou kind Father, God! Gladden our hearts through the fragrance of Thy love. Brighten our eyes through the Light of Thy Guidance. Delight our ears with the melody of Thy Word, and shelter us all in the Stronghold of Thy Providence.

Thou art the Mighty and Powerful, Thou art the Forgiving and Thou art the One Who overlooketh the shortcomings of all mankind.　**4**

O my God! O my God! Verily, I invoke Thee and supplicate before Thy threshold, asking Thee that all Thy mercies may descend upon these souls. Specialize them for Thy favor and Thy truth.

O Lord! Unite and bind together the hearts, join in accord all the souls, and exhilarate the spirits through the signs of Thy sanctity and oneness. O Lord! Make these faces radiant through the light of Thy oneness. Strengthen the loins of Thy servants in the service of Thy kingdom.

O Lord, Thou possessor of infinite mercy! O Lord of forgiveness and pardon! Forgive our sins, pardon our shortcomings, and cause us to turn to the kingdom of Thy clemency, invoking the kingdom of might and power, humble at Thy shrine and submissive before the glory of Thine evidences.

O Lord God! Make us as waves of the sea, as flowers of the garden, united, agreed through the bounties of Thy love. O Lord! Dilate the breasts through the signs of Thy oneness, and make all mankind as stars shining from the same height of glory, as perfect fruits growing upon Thy tree of life.

Verily, Thou art the Almighty, the Self-Subsistent, the Giver, the Forgiving, the Pardoner, the Omniscient, the One Creator. 5

Women

MEDITATION

The world of humanity is possessed of two wings: the male and the female. So long as these two wings are not equivalent in strength, the bird will not fly. Until womankind reaches the same degree as man, until she enjoys the same arena of activity, extraordinary attainment for humanity will not be realized; humanity cannot wing its way to heights of real attainment. When the two wings or parts become equivalent in strength, enjoying the same prerogatives, the flight of man will be exceedingly lofty and extraordinary. 1

PRAYERS

Glory to Thee, O my God! One of Thy hand-maidens, who hath believed in Thee and in Thy signs, hath entered beneath the shadow of the tree of Thy oneness. Give her to quaff, O my God, by Thy Name, the Manifest and the Hidden, of Thy choice sealed Wine that it may take her away from her own self, and make her to be entirely devoted to Thy remembrance, and wholly detached from any one beside Thee.

Now that Thou hast revealed unto her the knowledge of Thee, O my Lord, deny her not, by Thy bounty, Thy grace; and now that Thou hast called her unto Thyself, drive her not away from Thee, through Thy favor. Supply her, then, with that which excelleth all that can be found on Thine earth. Thou art, verily, the Most Bountiful, Whose grace is immense.

Wert Thou to bestow on one of Thy creatures what would equal the kingdoms of earth and heaven, it would still not diminish by even as much as an atom the immensity of Thy dominion. Far greater art Thou than the Great One men are wont to call Thee, for such a title is but one of Thy names all of which were created by a mere indication of Thy will.

There is no God but Thee, the God of power, the God of glory, the God of knowledge and wisdom.   2

Magnified be Thy name, O Lord my God! Behold Thou mine eye expectant to gaze on the wonders of Thy mercy, and mine ear longing to hearken unto Thy sweet melodies, and my heart yearning for the living waters of Thy knowledge. Thou seest Thy handmaiden, O my God, standing before the habitation of Thy mercy, and calling upon Thee by Thy name which Thou hast chosen above all other names and set up over all that are in heaven and on earth. Send down upon her the breaths of Thy mercy, that she may be carried away wholly from herself, and be drawn entirely towards the seat which, resplendent with the glory of Thy face, sheddeth afar the radiance of Thy sovereignty, and is established as Thy throne. Potent art Thou to do what Thou willest. No God is there beside Thee, the All-Glorious, the Most Bountiful.

Cast not out, I entreat Thee, O my Lord, them that have sought Thee, and turn not away such as have directed their steps towards Thee, and deprive not of Thy grace all that love Thee. Thou art He, O my Lord, Who hath called Himself the God of Mercy, the Most Compassionate. Have mercy, then, upon Thy handmaiden who hath sought Thy shelter, and set her face towards Thee.

Thou art, verily, the Ever-Forgiving, the Most Merciful.   3

O my Lord, my Beloved, my Desire! Befriend me in my loneliness and accompany me in my exile. Remove my sorrow. Cause me to be devoted to Thy beauty. Withdraw me from all else save Thee. Attract me through Thy fragrances of holiness. Cause me to be associated in Thy Kingdom with those who are severed from all else save Thee, who long to serve Thy sacred threshold and who stand to work in Thy Cause. Enable me to be one of Thy maidservants who have attained to Thy good pleasure. Verily, Thou art the Gracious, the Generous.   4

Youth

MEDITATIONS

Blessed is he who in the prime of his youth and the heyday of his life will arise to serve the Cause of the Lord of the beginning and of the end, and adorn his heart with His love. The manifestation of such a grace is greater than the creation of the heavens and of the earth. Blessed are the steadfast and well is it with those who are firm. 1

How to attain spirituality is, indeed, a question to which every young man and woman must sooner or later try to find a satisfactory answer. It is precisely because no such satisfactory reply has been given or found, that modern youth finds itself bewildered, and is being consequently carried away by the materialistic forces that are so powerfully undermining the foundation of man's moral and spiritual life. 2

PRAYERS

O Lord! Make this youth radiant, and confer Thy bounty upon this poor creature.
Bestow upon him knowledge, grant him added
strength at the break of every morn and guard him
within the shelter of Thy protection so that he
may be freed from error, may devote himself to
the service of Thy Cause, may guide the wayward,
lead the hapless, free the captives and awaken the
heedless, that all may be blessed with Thy remembrance and praise. Thou art the Mighty and the
Powerful.   3

O Thou Lord of wondrous grace! Bestow
upon us new blessings. Give to us the freshness of the spring. We are saplings which have
been planted by the fingers of Thy bounty and
have been formed out of the water and clay of
Thy tender affection. We thirst for the living
waters of Thy favors and are dependent upon the
outpourings of the clouds of Thy generosity.
Abandon not to itself this grove wherein our
hopes aspire, nor withhold therefrom the showers of Thy loving-kindness. Grant that from the

clouds of Thy mercy may fall copious rain so that the trees of our lives may bring forth fruit and we may attain the most cherished desire of our hearts.   **4**

Notes

INTRODUCTION

1. *Encyclopaedia Britannica* 15:948; Kahlil Gibran, *The Prophet,* p. 67; William James, *The Varieties of Religious Experience,* p. 464.

2. Bahá'u'lláh, *Hidden Words,* Arabic, nos. 3, 4, 5.

3. Psalms 42:2 RSV; *Confessions of Saint Augustine,* p. 6; Koran 3:20 (Rodwell).

4. 'Abdu'l-Bahá, in *Spiritual Foundations,* no. 34.

5. Bahá'u'lláh, *Kitáb-i-Íqán,* p. 238.

6. The Báb, *Selections,* p. 28; Bahá'u'lláh, *Kitáb-i-Aqdas,* para. 149.

7. 'Abdu'l-Bahá, *Selections,* no. 18:3.

8. Bahá'u'lláh, in *Bahá'í Prayers,* p. 4.

9. Bahá'u'lláh, in *Bahá'í Prayers,* p. v.

10. Bahá'u'lláh, *Prayers and Meditations,* p. 22.

11. 'Abdu'l-Bahá, in *Bahá'í Prayers,* p. 23.

12. Bahá'u'lláh, in *Bahá'í Prayers,* p. 87; 'Abdu'l-Bahá, *Selections,* no. 133:1.

13. Bahá'u'lláh, *Tablets,* p. 24; Bahá'u'lláh, in *Bahá'í Prayers,* p. 162.

14. The Báb, *Selections,* p. 178.

15. Bahá'u'lláh, *Prayers and Meditations,* p. 13.

16. Bahá'u'lláh, in *Bahá'í Prayers,* p. 204.

17. The Báb, in *Bahá'í Prayers,* p. 28.

18. Derrick Bell, *Gospel Choirs,* p. 1.

19. *An African Prayer Book,* p. xviii.

20. Extract from a letter written on behalf of Shoghi Effendi, in *Spiritual Foundations,* no. 40.

21. 'Abdu'l-Bahá, *Promulgation of Universal Peace,* p. 246; William and Madeline Hellaby, *Prayer,* pp. 75, 80.

22. 'Abdu'l-Bahá, *Selections,* no. 139:7–8.

23. 'Abdu'l-Bahá, *Some Answered Questions,* p. 224.

24. 'Abdu'l-Bahá, *Paris Talks,* no. 26:7.

25. Gerald O. Barney, *Threshold 2000,* p. 157.

26. Pope John Paul II, *A Pilgrim Pope,* p. 296.

27. 'Abdu'l-Bahá, in *Bahá'í Prayers,* p. 102.

28. Martin Luther King, Jr., in *The Wisdom of Martin Luther King, Jr.,* p. 162.

29. 'Abdu'l-Bahá, *Paris Talks,* no. 41:7.

ACCEPTING GOD'S WILL

1. 'Abdu'l-Bahá, *Selections,* no. 22:1.

2. On behalf of Shoghi Effendi, extract from a letter dated 30 October 1951, in *Light of Divine Guidance* 2:102.

3. Bahá'u'lláh, in *Prayers and Meditations,* pp. 240–42.

4. The Báb, in *Bahá'í Prayers,* p. 166.

CHILDREN

1. 'Abdu'l-Bahá, *Selections,* no. 110:3.

2. 'Abdu'l-Bahá, *Selections,* no. 99:1.

3. Bahá'u'lláh, in *Bahá'í Prayers,* p. 34.

4. Bahá'u'lláh, *Prayers and Meditations,* pp. 236–37.

5. 'Abdu'l-Bahá, in *Bahá'í Prayers,* p. 35.

6. 'Abdu'l-Bahá, in *Bahá'í Prayers,* p. 35.

7. 'Abdu'l-Bahá, in *Bahá'í Prayers,* pp. 35–36.

8. 'Abdu'l-Bahá, in *Bahá'í Prayers,* p. 36.

9. 'Abdu'l-Bahá, in *Bahá'í Prayers,* pp. 36–37.
10. 'Abdu'l-Bahá, in *Bahá'í Prayers,* pp. 37–38.
11. 'Abdu'l-Bahá, in *Bahá'í Prayers,* p. 38.
12. 'Abdu'l-Bahá, in *O God! My God!* no. 24.

COMFORT
1. 'Abdu'l-Bahá, *Paris Talks,* no. 35:8–10.
2. The Báb, in *Bahá'í Prayers,* p. 29.
3. 'Abdu'l-Bahá, in *Bahá'í Prayers,* p. 24.

CONTENTMENT
1. Bahá'u'lláh, *Tablets,* p. 155.
2. 'Abdu'l-Bahá, *Paris Talks,* no. 35:12.
3. Bahá'u'lláh, in *Bahá'í Prayers,* pp. 143–44.
4. The Báb, in *Bahá'í Prayers,* pp. 56–57.

THE DEPARTED
1. Bahá'u'lláh, *Gleanings,* p. 345.
2. Bahá'u'lláh, *Gleanings,* p. 155.
3. 'Abdu'l-Bahá, *Paris Talks,* no. 20:6.
4. 'Abdu'l-Bahá, *Paris Talks,* no. 29:8.
5. Bahá'u'lláh, in *Bahá'í Prayers,* pp. 41–42.
6. 'Abdu'l-Bahá, in *Bahá'í Prayers,* pp. 45–46.
7. 'Abdu'l-Bahá, in *Bahá'í Prayers,* pp. 46–47.

DETACHMENT
1. Bahá'u'lláh, *Hidden Words,* Persian, no. 51.
2. 'Abdu'l-Bahá, *Paris Talks,* no. 28:19.
3. The Báb, in *Bahá'í Prayers,* p. 29.
4. The Báb, in *Bahá'í Prayers,* p. 22.
5. 'Abdu'l-Bahá, in *Bahá'í Prayers,* pp. 152–53.

DIFFICULT TIMES

1. 'Abdu'l-Bahá, *Selections*, no. 150:3.

2. On behalf of Shoghi Effendi, extract from a letter dated 29 May 1935, in *Unfolding Destiny*, p. 434.

3. Bahá'u'lláh, in *Bahá'í Prayers*, pp. 27–28.

4. Bahá'u'lláh, in *Bahá'í Prayers*, p. 191.

5. The Báb, in *Bahá'í Prayers*, pp. 194–95.

6. The Báb, *Selections*, pp. 204–05.

7. The Báb, in *Bahá'í Prayers*, p. 28.

8. The Báb, *Selections*, pp. 205–06.

9. 'Abdu'l-Bahá, in *Bahá'í Prayers*, pp. 188–89.

EVENING

1. Bahá'u'lláh, *Kitáb-i-Aqdas*, para. 33.

2. 'Abdu'l-Bahá, *Selections*, no. 172:1.

3. Bahá'u'lláh, in *Bahá'í Prayers*, p. 60.

4. Bahá'u'lláh, in *Bahá'í Prayers*, pp. 60–61

5. 'Abdu'l-Bahá, in *Bahá'í Prayers*, pp. 61–62.

FAITH

1. Bahá'u'lláh, *Gleanings*, p. 234.

2. Bahá'u'lláh, *Tablets*, p. 156.

3. 'Abdu'l-Bahá, *Paris Talks*, no. 34:8.

4. Bahá'u'lláh, in *Bahá'í Prayers*, pp. 161–62.

5. 'Abdu'l-Bahá, in *Bahá'í Prayers*, p. 167.

6. 'Abdu'l-Bahá, in *Bahá'í Prayers*, pp. 71–72.

FORGIVENESS

1. The Báb, *Selections*, pp. 19–20.

2. 'Abdu'l-Bahá, *Selections*, no. 82:1.

3. The Báb, in *Bahá'í Prayers*, pp. 79–80.

4. The Báb, in *Bahá'í Prayers*, p. 80.

5. The Báb, in *Bahá'í Prayers*, p. 81.

6. The Báb, in *Bahá'í Prayers*, pp. 81–82.

7. The Báb, *Selections*, p. 182.

8. 'Abdu'l-Bahá, in *Bahá'í Prayers*, p. 47.

9. 'Abdu'l-Bahá, *Promulgation of Universal Peace*, p. 176.

GUIDANCE AND INSPIRATION

1. Bahá'u'lláh, *Gleanings*, p. 267.

2. Bahá'u'lláh quoted in Shoghi Effendi, *Advent of Divine Justice*, p. 76.

3. Bahá'u'lláh, *Tablets*, pp. 268–69.

4. 'Abdu'l-Bahá, in *Bahá'í Prayers*, p. 103.

5. 'Abdu'l-Bahá, in *Bahá'í Prayers*, p. 37.

HAPPINESS

1. Bahá'u'lláh, *Kitáb-i-Aqdas*, para. 149.

2. 'Abdu'l-Bahá, *Paris Talks*, no. 23:7.

3. 'Abdu'l-Bahá, *Selections*, no. 100:2.

4. 'Abdu'l-Bahá, *Promulgation of Universal Peace*, p. 468.

5. 'Abdu'l-Bahá, in *Bahá'í Prayers*, pp. 57–58.

6. 'Abdu'l-Bahá, in *Bahá'í Prayers*, p. 152.

HEALING

1. Bahá'u'lláh, *Gleanings*, pp. 153–54.

2. 'Abdu'l-Bahá, *Selections*, no. 133:1.

3. Bahá'u'lláh, in *Bahá'í Prayers*, p. 87.

4. Bahá'u'lláh, in *Bahá'í Prayers*, p. 86.

HELP AND ASSISTANCE

1. 'Abdu'l-Bahá, in *Spiritual Foundations,* no. 25.

2. 'Abdu'l-Bahá, *Paris Talks,* no. 9:24–25.

3. On behalf of Shoghi Effendi, extract from a letter dated 4 May 1942, in *Power of Divine Assistance,* p. 53.

4. Bahá'u'lláh, *Tablets of Bahá'u'lláh,* pp. 95–96.

5. Bahá'u'lláh, *Epistle,* pp. 70–71.

6. The Báb, in *Bahá'í Prayers,* pp. 55–56.

7. The Báb, in *Bahá'í Prayers,* pp. 132–33.

8. 'Abdu'l-Bahá, in *Bahá'í Prayers,* pp. 23–24.

9. 'Abdu'l-Bahá, in *Bahá'í Prayers,* pp. 30–31.

HOME

1. 'Abdu'l-Bahá, in *Family Life,* p. 8

2. Bahá'u'lláh, in *Bahá'í Prayers,* p. iii.

HOPE

1. 'Abdu'l-Bahá, *Selections,* no. 178:1.

2. 'Abdu'l-Bahá, *Selections,* no. 35:10.

3. Bahá'u'lláh, in *Bahá'í Prayers,* pp. 141–42.

4. 'Abdu'l-Bahá, in *Bahá'í Prayers,* pp. 31–32.

HUMANITY

1. 'Abdu'l-Bahá, *Promulgation of Universal Peace,* p. 297.

2. 'Abdu'l-Bahá, *Promulgation of Universal Peace,* p. 118.

3. Bahá'u'lláh, in *Bahá'í Prayers* (U.K. ed.), pp. 60–61.

4. The Báb, *Selections,* p. 191.

5. 'Abdu'l-Bahá, in *Bahá'í Prayers,* p. 100.

6. 'Abdu'l-Bahá, in *Bahá'í Prayers,* pp. 100–01.

7. 'Abdu'l-Bahá, *Selections,* no. 2:10–11.

HUMILITY

1. Bahá'u'lláh, *Tablets,* p. 64.

2. Bahá'u'lláh, *Epistle,* p. 44.

3. 'Abdu'l-Bahá, *Promulgation of Universal Peace,* p. 63.

4. Bahá'u'lláh, in *Bahá'í Prayers,* p. 4.

5. Bahá'u'lláh, in *Bahá'í Prayers,* pp. 77–78.

6. The Báb, in *Bahá'í Prayers,* pp. 150–51.

LOVED ONES

1. 'Abdu'l-Bahá, *Paris Talks,* no. 9:21.

2. 'Abdu'l-Bahá, *Promulgation of Universal Peace,* p. 93.

3. Bahá'u'lláh, *Prayers and Meditations,* pp. 195–96.

4. Bahá'u'lláh, in *Bahá'í Prayers,* pp. 124–25.

5. The Báb, in *Bahá'í Prayers,* pp. 64–65.

6. 'Abdu'l-Bahá, in *Bahá'í Prayers,* pp. 65–66.

MARRIAGE

1. 'Abdu'l-Bahá, *Selections,* no. 92:1–2.

2. 'Abdu'l-Bahá, in *Bahá'í Prayers,* pp. 105–06.

3. 'Abdu'l-Bahá, in *Bahá'í Prayers,* p. 107.

MATERIAL NEEDS

1. Bahá'u'lláh, *Gleanings,* p. 276.

2. Bahá'u'lláh, in *Bahá'í Prayers,* pp. 26–27.

3. 'Abdu'l-Bahá, in *Bahá'í Prayers,* pp. 84–85.

4. 'Abdu'l-Bahá, in *Bahá'í Prayers,* pp. 22–23.

MEETINGS AND GATHERINGS

1. 'Abdu'l-Bahá, *Selections*, no. 56:1.
2. 'Abdu'l-Bahá, in *Bahá'í Prayers*, pp. 155–56.
3. 'Abdu'l-Bahá, in *Bahá'í Prayers*, pp. 156–58.
4. 'Abdu'l-Bahá, in *Bahá'í Prayres*, pp. 82–83.
5. 'Abdu'l-Bahá, in *Bahá'í Prayers*, pp. 110–11.
6. 'Abdu'l-Bahá, in *Bahá'í Prayers*, pp. 111–12.
7. 'Abdu'l-Bahá, in *Bahá'í Prayers*, pp. 112–13.

MORNING

1. Bahá'u'lláh, *Kitáb-i-Aqdas*, para. 33.
2. Bahá'u'lláh, *Tablets*, p. 138.
3. 'Abdu'l-Bahá, *Selections*, no. 59:3.
4. Bahá'u'lláh, in *Bahá'í Prayers*, p. 117.
5. Bahá'u'lláh, in *Bahá'í Prayers*, p. 118.

NEARNESS TO GOD

1. Bahá'u'lláh, *Tablets*, p. 155.
2. 'Abdu'l-Bahá, *Promulgation of Universal Peace*, p. 148.
3. Bahá'u'lláh, in *Bahá'í Prayers*, pp. 144–45.
4. Bahá'u'lláh, in *Bahá'í Prayers*, pp. 162–63.
5. Bahá'u'lláh, in *Bahá'í Prayers*, pp. 78–79.
6. Bahá'u'lláh, in *Bahá'í Prayers*, pp. 52–53.
7. Bahá'u'lláh, in *Bahá'í Prayers*, pp. 48–49.
8. 'Abdu'l-Bahá, in *Bahá'í Prayers*, pp. 153–54.

PRAISE AND GRATITUDE

1. Bahá'u'lláh, *Kitáb-i-Aqdas*, para. 40.
2. 'Abdu'l-Bahá, *Selections*, no. 153:1.
3. Bahá'u'lláh, in *Bahá'í Prayers*, p. 99.

4. Bahá'u'lláh, in *Bahá'í Prayers*, pp. 122–23.
5. Bahá'u'lláh, in *Bahá'í Prayers*, pp. 121–22.
6. Bahá'u'lláh, in *Bahá'í Prayers*, pp. 19–20.
7. The Báb, in *Bahá'í Prayers*, pp. 126–27.
8. The Báb, in *Bahá'í Prayers*, pp. 20–22.
9. 'Abdu'l-Bahá, in *Bahá'í Prayers*, pp. 167–68.

PROTECTION

1. The Báb, *Selections*, p. 172.
2. The Báb, *Selections*, p. 171.
3. 'Abdu'l-Bahá, *Paris Talks*, no. 9:25.
4. Bahá'u'lláh, in *Bahá'í Prayers*, p. 131.
5. Bahá'u'lláh, in *Bahá'í Prayers*, pp. 129–30.
6. Bahá'u'lláh, in *Bahá'í Prayers*, pp. 193–94.
7. The Báb, in *Bahá'í Prayers*, p. 29.
8. 'Abdu'l-Bahá, in *Bahá'í Prayers*, p. 136.

PURITY

1. Bahá'u'lláh, *Epistle*, p. 131.
2. 'Abdu'l-Bahá, *'Abdu'l-Bahá in London*, p. 107.
3. 'Abdu'l-Bahá, *Selections*, no. 129:3–4.
4. Bahá'u'lláh, in *Bahá'í Prayers*, pp. 142–43.
5. 'Abdu'l-Bahá, in *Bahá'í Prayers*, pp. 37.

SHARING GOD'S LOVE

1. 'Abdu'l-Bahá, *Paris Talks*, no. 5:24.
2. 'Abdu'l-Bahá, *Paris Talks*, no. 1:7.
3. Bahá'u'lláh, in *Bahá'í Prayers*, pp. 173–74.
4. 'Abdu'l-Bahá, in *Bahá'í Prayers*, p. 115.
5. 'Abdu'l-Bahá, in *Bahá'í Prayers*, pp. 174–75.

SPIRITUAL GROWTH

1. Bahá'u'lláh, quoted in Shoghi Effendi, *Advent of Divine Justice*, p. 26.

2. On behalf of Shoghi Effendi, extract from a letter dated 5 August 1949, in *Bahá'í News*, no. 231, p. 1.

3. Bahá'u'lláh, in *Bahá'í Prayers*, p. 146.

4. Bahá'u'lláh, in *Bahá'í Prayers*, p. 19.

5. Bahá'u'lláh, in *Bahá'í Prayers*, pp. 149–50.

6. 'Abdu'l-Bahá, in *Bahá'í Prayers*, pp. 135–36.

7. 'Abdu'l-Bahá, in *Bahá'í Prayers*, pp. 187–88.

8. 'Abdu'l-Bahá, in *Bahá'í Prayers*, p. 153.

9. 'Abdu'l-Bahá, *Selections*, no. 2:2–5.

STRENGTH

1. Bahá'u'lláh, *Tablets*, p. 156.

2. 'Abdu'l-Bahá, quoted in Shoghi Effendi, *Advent of Divine Justice*, p. 62.

3. On behalf of Shoghi Effendi, extract from a letter dated 14 February 1925, in *Lights of Guidance*, no. 1378.

4. Bahá'u'lláh, in *Bahá'í Prayers*, pp. 145–46.

5. Bahá'u'lláh, in *Bahá'í Prayers*, pp. 160–61.

UNITY

1. Bahá'u'lláh, *Tablets*, p. 167.

2. Bahá'u'lláh, *Tablets*, p. 168.

3. Bahá'u'lláh, in *Bahá'í Prayers*, p. 204.

4. 'Abdu'l-Bahá, in *Bahá'í Prayers*, pp. 101–02.

5. 'Abdu'l-Bahá, in *Bahá'í Prayers*, pp. 204–05.

Women

1. 'Abdu'l-Bahá, *Promulgation of Universal Peace,* p. 375.

2. Bahá'u'lláh, in *Prayers and Meditations,* pp. 156–57.

3. Bahá'u'lláh, in *Prayers and Meditations,* pp. 147–48.

4. 'Abdu'l-Bahá, in *Bahá'í Prayers,* pp. 32–33.

Youth

1. Bahá'u'lláh, in *Youth,* no. 1.

2. On behalf of Shoghi Effendi, extract from a letter dated 8 December 1935, in *Youth,* no. 30.

3. 'Abdu'l-Bahá, in *Bahá'í Prayers,* p. 39.

4. 'Abdu'l-Bahá, in *O God! My God!,* no. 33.

Bibliography

Works of Bahá'u'lláh

Epistle to the Son of the Wolf. Translated by Shoghi Effendi. 1st pocket-size ed. Wilmette, Ill.: Bahá'í Publishing Trust, 1988.

Gleanings from the Writings of Bahá'u'lláh. Translated by Shoghi Effendi. 1st pocket-size ed. Wilmette, Ill.: Bahá'í Publishing Trust, 1983.

The Hidden Words. Translated by Shoghi Effendi. Wilmette, Ill.: Bahá'í Publishing Trust, 1939.

The Kitáb-i-Aqdas: The Most Holy Book. 1st pocket-size ed. Wilmette, Ill: Bahá'í Publishing Trust, 1993.

Prayers and Meditations. Translated by Shoghi Effendi. 1st pocket-size ed. Wilmette, Ill.: Bahá'í Publishing Trust, 1987.

Tablets of Bahá'u'lláh revealed after the Kitáb-i-Aqdas. Compiled by the Research Department of the Universal House of Justice. Translated by Habib Taherzadeh et al. Wilmette, Ill.: Bahá'í Publishing Trust, 1988.

Works of the Báb

Selections from the Writings of the Báb. Compiled by the Research Department of the Universal House of Justice. Translated by Habib Taherzadeh et al. Haifa: Bahá'í World Centre, 1976.

WORKS OF 'ABDU'L-BAHÁ

'Abdu'l-Bahá in London: Addresses and Notes of Conversations. [Compiled by Eric Hammond.] London: Longmans Green, 1912; repr. London: Bahá'í Publishing Trust, 1982.

Paris Talks: Addresses Given by 'Abdu'l-Bahá in 1911. 12th ed. London: Bahá'í Publishing Trust, 1995.

The Promulgation of Universal Peace: Talks Delivered by 'Abdu'l-Bahá during His Visit to the United States and Canada in 1912. Compiled by Howard MacNutt. 2d ed. Wilmette, Ill.: Bahá'í Publishing Trust, 1982.

Selections from the Writings of 'Abdu'l-Bahá. Compiled by the Research Department of the Universal House of Justice. Translated by a Committee at the Bahá'í World Center and by Marzieh Gail. Wilmette, Ill.: Bahá'í Publishing Trust, 1997.

OTHER WORKS

Alex Ayres, ed. *The Wisdom of Martin Luther King, Jr.* New York: Meridian, 1993.

Bahá'í News, no. 231 (May 1950): 1.

Bahá'í Prayers: A Selection of Prayers Revealed by Bahá'u'lláh, the Báb, and 'Abdu'l-Bahá. New ed. Wilmette, Ill.: Bahá'í Publishing Trust, 1991.

Bahá'u'lláh and 'Abdu'l-Bahá. *O God, My God . . . : Bahá'í Prayers and Tablets for Children and Youth.* Text in English and Persian. Wilmette, Ill.: Bahá'í Publishing Trust, 1984.

[Bahá'u'lláh, the Báb, and 'Abdu'l-Bahá]. *Bahá'í Prayers: A Selection.* Rev. ed. London: Bahá'í Publishing Trust, 1975.

Bahá'u'lláh, the Báb, 'Abdu'l-Bahá, and Shoghi Effendi. *The Power of Divine Assistance.* Compiled by the Research Department of the Universal House of Justice. N.p.: National Spiritual Assembly of Canada, 1982.

[Bahá'u'lláh, the Báb, 'Abdu'l-Bahá, Shoghi Effendi, and the Universal House of Justice.] *Family Life.* Compiled by the Research Department of the Universal House of Justice. Oakham, U.K: Bahá'í Publishing Trust, 1982.

Barney, Gerald O. *Threshold 2000: Critical Issues and Spiritual Values for a Global Age,* for the Parliament of World's Religions. Ada, MI: CoNexus Press, 2000.

Bell, Derrick. *Gospel Choirs: Psalms of Survival in an Alien Land Called Home*. New York: BasicBooks, 1996.

Confessions of Saint Augustine. Translated by Edward B. Pusey, D.D. New York: Modern Library, 1999

Gibran, Kahlil. *The Prophet*. New York: Alfred A. Knopf, 1971.

Hellaby, William and Madeline. *Prayer: A Bahá'í Approach*. Oxford, U.K.: George Ronald, 1986.

James, William. *The Varieties of Religious Experience: A Study in Human Nature*. Edited with an introduction by Martin E. Marty. New York: Penguin Books, 1982; repr. 1985.

Lights of Guidance: A Bahá'í Reference File. Compiled by Helen Hornby. 6th ed. New Delhi: Bahá'í Publishing Trust, 1999.

Pope John Paul II. *A Pilgrim Pope: Messages for the World*. Edited by Cardinal Achille Silvestrini with the assistance of Jerome M. Vereb, C.P. Foreword by Cardinal Pio Laghi. Kansas City, MO: K. S. Giniger Company, in association with Andrews McMeel Publishing, 1999.

"Prayer." *Encyclopaedia Britannica Macropaedia*, vol. 14. Chicago: University of Chicago, 1980.

Shoghi Effendi. *The Advent of Divine Justice*. 1st pocket-size ed. Wilmette, Ill.: Bahá'í Publishing Trust, 1990.

————. *The Light of Divine Guidance: Letters from the Guardian of the Bahá'í Faith to Individual Believers, Groups and Bahá'í Communities in Germany and Austria*. Langenhain, West Germany: National Spiritual Assembly of the Bahá'ís of Germany, 1985.

Spiritual Foundations: Prayer, Meditation, and the Devotional Attitude: Extracts from the Writings of Bahá'u'lláh, 'Abdu'l-Bahá, and Shoghi Effendi. Compiled by the Research Department of the Universal House of Justice. Wilmette, Ill.: Bahá'í Publishing Trust, 1980.

Tutu, Desmond, ed. *An African Prayer Book*. New York: Doubleday, 1995.

Shoghi Effendi. *The Unfolding Destiny of the British Bahá'í Community: The Messages from the Guardian of the Bahá'í Faith to the Baha'is of the British Isles*. London: Bahá'í Publishing Trust, 1981.

Youth: Extracts from the Writings of Bahá'u'lláh, 'Abdu'l-Bahá and Shoghi Effendi. Compiled by the Research Department of the Universal House of Justice. Mona Vale, Australia: Bahá'í Publications Australia, 1995.

Alphabetical Index to
First Lines of Prayers

General Index

About the Bahá'í Faith

In just over one hundred years the Bahá'í Faith has grown from an obscure movement in the Middle East to the second-most widespread independent world religion after Christianity. With some 5 million adherents in virtually every corner of the globe—including people from every nation, ethnic group, culture, profession, and social or economic class—it is probably the most diverse organized body of people on the planet today.

Its founder, Bahá'u'lláh, teaches that there is only one God, that there is only one human race, and that all the world's major religions have been stages in the progressive revelation of God's purpose for humankind. Bahá'ís believe that the unity of the entire human race is not only necessary for human progress but also inevitable. The Bahá'í Faith teaches, among other things, that religion should be a source of unity; condemns all forms of prejudice and racism; upholds the equality of women and men; confirms the importance and value of marriage and the family; establishes the need for the independent investigation of the truth; insists on access to education for all; asserts the essential harmony between science and religion; declares the need to eliminate extremes of wealth and poverty; and exalts work done in a spirit of service to the level of worship.

Bahá'ís believe that religion should be a dynamic force that raises the individual, family, and community to new spiritual heights. To this end Bahá'ís all around the world work to create an atmosphere of love and unity in their own lives, in their families, and in their communities.

For more information about the Bahá'í Faith, visit

http://www.us.bahai.org/

or call

1-800-22-UNITE.

About
Bahá'í Publishing

Bahá'í Publishing produces books based on the teachings of the Bahá'í Faith, a worldwide religious community united by the belief that there is one God, one human race, and one evolving religion.

For more than a century, Bahá'í communities around the globe have been working to break down barriers of prejudice between peoples and have collaborated with other like-minded groups to promote the model of a global society. At the heart of Bahá'í teachings is the conviction that humanity is a single people with a common destiny. In the words of Bahá'u'lláh, the Founder of the Bahá'í Faith, "The earth is but one country, and mankind its citizens."

Today the Bahá'í Faith is among the fastest growing of the world religions. With some 5 million followers in virtually every country and dependent territory, it has already become the second-most widespread of the world's faiths, surpassing every religion but Christianity in its geographic reach.

Bahá'í Publishing is an imprint of the Bahá'í Publishing Trust of the United States.

Other Books Available from Bahá'í Publishing

SEEKING FAITH:
IS RELIGION REALLY WHAT YOU THINK IT IS?

by Nathan Rutstein

What does religion mean to you? How do you develop a greater sense of purpose in life? How can you cultivate your own spiritual growth? And how do you know if you're heading down the right path? For many people religion is the answer. But what is *true* religion, and how do you know when you've found it?

Nathan Rutstein provides a personal, thoughtful exploration of these and other questions. At a time when many are struggling with life's most difficult questions, *Seeking Faith* offers a hopeful perspective for the future. It explores how to find your true purpose and create peace and happiness in your own life as well as in the world around you, no matter who you are and no matter what circumstances affect you.

A Wayfarer's Guide to Bringing the Sacred Home

by Joseph Sheppherd

A spiritual journey to find the sacred within ourselves and those around us. What is the spiritual connection between self, family, and community? What do these relationships have to do with our spiritual development? In this engaging work about the importance of bringing spiritual values to everyday living, Joseph Sheppherd explores issues that shape our lives and the lives of those around us: the vital role of personal transformation in spiritual growth, the importance of spiritual training in raising children, the divine purpose of marriage and family, and processes for building strong communities. Offering a means to bring hope, joy, and meaning to a challenged world, this is an enlightening guide for anyone seeking spiritual fulfillment in their personal life, their family life, or the life of their community.

Available through bookstores everywhere.